privilege of working closely with Pradeep and have seen the dedication he has to his craft and the emphasis he lays on teamwork, which is what helps him deliver results that other pollsters can only dream of. This work ethic is also what gives me the confidence of running his exit poll results on the India Today Group even if they so against the grain of perceived wisdom about which way the "hawa" is blowing.'
Kalli Purie, Vice Chairperson, India Today Group

'An Indian election verdict is often a puzzle wrapped in a mystery. But how do you make sense of the numbers? No pollster does that better than Pradeep Gupta, the man who gets it right more often than anyone else. *How India Votes* tries to decode the science behind the maths of exit polling. Valuable reading for anyone who wants to understand an Indian election and exit polling.'
Rajdeep Sardesai

Praise for the Book

'Axis My India has predicted the results of most elections accurately. This shows their ability to understand the mind and the expectations of the common man of this country.

Pradeep Gupta is one of the most well-known psephologists of India and he has studied the social, economic and political realities of the country very thoroughly. Through his in-depth surveys and studies, he has developed a great insight into the voter's psychology and election results.

I am very confident that this book will prove to be helpful for both voters and election analysts in developing the right understanding of how people use their right to vote and how election results should be analysed.'
Amit Shah, Union Minister of Home Affairs

'Pradeep Gupta and Axis My India are pioneers in conducting election surveys and gauging the public mood. He is well known for conducting data-based scientific surveys all over the country. I believe his success comes from his deep understanding of the voter's psychology which goes beyond market research and statistics.

In *How India Votes*, Pradeep Gupta delves deep into the psyche of the Indian voter and takes readers on an insightful journey through how Indians choose their leaders.'
Y.S. Jagan Mohan Reddy, Chief Minister of Andhra Pradesh

'Pradeep Gupta of Axis My India has been doing election-related surveys all over India for almost a decade. He has turned this huge experience into the book *How India Votes*. I hope this book proves to be very useful to election experts in understanding the people and voting culture of the world's largest democracy.'
Shivraj Singh Chouhan, Chief Minister of Madhya Pradesh

'Why do people vote the way they do? Pradeep Gupta uses data obtained from Axis My India's rigorous surveys of Indian voters to explain what motivates – and what does not appear to matter to – Indian voters. He draws significantly on data gathered during Axis My India's survey of Indian voters. Axis My India's processes are documented in a Harvard Business School case on the company. This book is vital for anyone interested in how Indian democracy works and has important lessons for those interested in how democracy works in other parts of the world.'
Ananth Raman, UPS Foundation Professor of Business Logistics, Harvard Business School

'Pradeep Gupta is the gold standard of polling in India. His pioneering technique of conducting a post-poll study in every seat allows for a granular understanding of election results. Axis My India's enviable track record has transformed how opinion polling is perceived in the country. I have had the

How India Votes

How India Votes

And What It Means

Pradeep Gupta

JUGGERNAUT BOOKS
C-I-128, First Floor, Sangam Vihar, Near Holi Chowk,
New Delhi 110080, India

First published in hardback by Juggernaut Books 2021
Published in paperback 2022

Copyright © Pradeep Gupta 2021
Foreword to the Paperback Edition copyright © Pradeep Gupta 2022
Appendix: 2021 – Assembly Election copyright
© Pradeep Gupta 2022

10 9 8 7 6 5 4 3 2 1

P-ISBN: 9789391165635
E-ISBN: 9789353451400

All rights reserved. No part of this publication may be reproduced, transmitted, or stored in a retrieval system in any form or by any means without the written permission of the publisher.

Typeset in Adobe Caslon Pro by R. Ajith Kumar, Noida

Printed at Thomson Press India Ltd

Contents

Foreword   xi

Introduction: Methodology   1

1. Election Results Will Move in One Direction – As a Result of Technology and Communications   17

2. Delivery, Delivery, Delivery   35

3. Women Emerging as an Important Vote Bank   49

4. Communalism   65

5. PM Contenders   79

6. Indian Poor Vote More Than the Rich   93

7. Dynasty Is Dead and Criminality Is Heading the Same Way   107

Contents

8. Crowds at Rallies Don't Mean Victory — 119
9. GDP and Stock Market Figures Have No Bearing on Poll Prospects — 131

Appendix: Axis My India – Track Record — 143
Acknowledgements — 171
A Note on the Author — 173

Foreword

A lot has changed since the first edition of this book came out.

In May, the Trinamool Congress (TMC) won a hard-fought victory in the West Bengal polls by defeating an aggressive Bharatiya Janata Party (BJP) campaign to wrest the state away. The result has set the cat among the pigeons in the Opposition camp, leading to some churning.

The year-long protests by farmers against the three central agricultural laws are also finally over, with the Modi government withdrawing the controversial laws in a rare retreat. Since first edition's release, the chief ministers of four states – Gujarat, Punjab, Uttarakhand and Karnataka – have been shunted.

Amidst all this, poll season is upon us again with Uttar Pradesh, Punjab, Uttarakhand, Goa, Manipur, Gujarat and Himachal Pradesh set to elect new governments in 2022. While Gujarat and Himachal

Pradesh will go to polls later this year, the other five will likely see elections in February and March.

Six of these seven states currently have a BJP government, with the Congress as its principal challenger. In many of these states, like Goa, Punjab and Uttarakhand, other parties are emerging as alternatives to both the principal parties. 2022, then, represents Congress' best chance to gain a foothold, re-establish its dominance and fend off other Opposition parties baying for a larger role.

The outcomes of each of these polls will be crucial in their own contexts, but the one that is surely going to indelibly alter the country's landscape, irrespective of the result, is the outcome of the Uttar Pradesh polls.

Unarguably, Uttar Pradesh is the most important state in the country for any political party's fortunes since it sends a total of eighty Lok Sabha and thirty-one Rajya Sabha MPs. But for pollsters like me, Uttar Pradesh, apart from being critical, is also a challenging state to crack.

First, the size.

Uttar Pradesh has the most number of legislative assembly constituencies at 403; for context, the state with the second-largest number of seats is West

Bengal with 294 seats. To get this state right, we employ nearly ten times as many personnel on the ground to conduct interviews. Even the time taken to conduct our surveys is a lot more than it is in other major states.

So vast is the state that the six different regions within it have varied, often contrasting, problems the populace keeps in mind while voting.

For instance, the infrastructural development in western Uttar Pradesh is on par with the infrastructure in some of the most progressive regions in other states, whereas eastern Uttar Pradesh, also known as Purvanchal, is one of the most under-developed territories in the country.

I remember asking residents in western Uttar Pradesh – most of whom are engaged in cultivating sugar cane – what their problems were, listing out basic amenities I thought they would choose from, like water supply, power and roads. They chose none of these and instead conveyed that the only issue they faced was the long pendency of their dues from the sugar cane crushing factories in the area. In stark contrast, locals in Purvanchal told us they were struggling for bare necessities like clean drinking water and quality healthcare services. Sugar cane played no role in people's voting choices there. In these parts, there are no jobs, whereas western Uttar Pradesh boasts of some of the biggest manufacturing units of global companies.

As a result, the needs of both these regions are often diametrically opposite.

Similarly, the proportion of its major castes also varies across different regions, making it difficult to predict their voting patterns. In the western part of the state, Muslims and Jats are dominant. In contrast, the Yadav community is dominant in central Uttar Pradesh. In the eastern part of Uttar Pradesh, upper-caste groups and Dalit communities are dominant, while the proportion of Muslims, Jats and Yadavs is too little to matter, with the exception of Azamgarh.

Another unique aspect is the abundance of smaller, regional and caste-specific parties in the state. From the Rashtriya Lok Dal to the Apna Dal, from the Nishad Party to the Suheldev Bharatiya Samaj Party, smaller parties are integral to Uttar Pradesh's electoral politics. While these parties might not win many seats on their strength, they can end up cutting into the votes of other parties. That is why, come election season, each major political player in Uttar Pradesh tries to lure some of these parties their way.

With such a vast and diverse electorate, it isn't entirely surprising that holding the reins of the state is also a tricky affair for its politicians.

Uttar Pradesh is one of the only states currently that has a four-corner contest in which all the four players – the BJP, the Congress, the Samajwadi Party and the Bahujan Samaj Party (BSP) – have come to power with a majority at least once in the last four decades and have formed alliance governments at least twice.

But what, in my view, truly shows why Uttar Pradesh can be tricky to predict is a fact that is often overlooked in popular discourse around this state's polity. It is that no ruling government in the last four decades has been able to get re-elected there despite getting handsome majorities in their first tenures. The last three governments formed in the state – in 2007, 2012 and 2017 – were all formed with full majorities, only for the incumbent to be booted out the next time. The electorate there is alert and watchful and doesn't mind relegating the most powerful of its chief ministers to political oblivion.

One often associates this nearly compulsive anti-incumbency with states like Punjab, Kerala and Tamil Nadu, but the Uttar Pradesh electorate can be as fickle, and trends could change at any time, making it an unpredictable election till the last vote is cast.

All this only makes our jobs as pollsters tougher.

Since our methodology at Axis My India involves surveying each seat, the Uttar Pradesh elections are a labourious effort, especially since the vast and diverse demography means that one cannot extrapolate any assumptions gathered in specific areas and regions. In other states, one gets a general voting pattern in the months leading up to the election, but in Uttar Pradesh, these trends change within a matter of weeks.

In most other states, apart from surveying each seat, we study the inclinations of five major caste groups towards the big political players to gather an accurate understanding of the voting trends. In Uttar Pradesh, we need to study at least fifteen castes and sub-castes to be able to develop a similar understanding.

The results of these polls are bound to have implications on the careers of some of the leading players.

For Yogi Adityanath, an outright victory would mean he would become the first chief minister in decades to be re-elected for a second term. Needless to say, such a victory would also cement his place in the pantheon of prominent Uttar Pradesh leaders.

For his main contender, Akhilesh Yadav, the poll is a test of his popularity and, to some measure, even his legacy. The results will tell us whether the electorate thinks of Yadav as a mass leader, like his father Mulayam Singh Yadav, and whether he can expand beyond his urban-centric image. For Mayawati, this election might be a win-or-bust poll, since she has already been out of power for ten years now. Her party is floundering, her resources seem depleted and her leaders are deserting her. Our experience on the ground tells us that her vote bank is committed to her, but that alone is unlikely to make a significant difference to her fortunes.

Priyanka Gandhi Vadra is leading the charge for the Congress, and the party's faring will be seen as a judgement on her. For years now, there has been some clamour around her entry into politics, with breathless followers even comparing her to grandmother Indira Gandhi. Her focus on female voters is novel, and the outcome will tell us whether this approach proved to be wise or not. This is the first full-fledged poll campaign she is in charge of;

it will be her first big test, and if she loses, her last because the failure might be difficult for her to shrug off.

Lastly, the polls will also be seen as a referendum on Modi's popularity. A loss will galvanize the Opposition and inflict a deep blow on the prime minister's repute as a leader, especially after the loss in Bengal; a win will only further cement his appeal.

As with these principal players, even the principal parties have a lot riding on these polls.

A crushing defeat for the Congress in these polls will cast a shadow on Gandhi Vadra's future as a leader and only increase the din among the Opposition parties for a stronger anchor to lead the alternative charge against the BJP. For the BJP, a win will reassure them of the party's re-election prospects come 2024. It could considerably deflate the Opposition's belief and morale – that the 2024 results will be different from the one of 2019.

All in all, the outcome of the Uttar Pradesh polls is likely to set the tone for the country's politics over the next two years.

Not too far away from Uttar Pradesh, the politicking in Punjab might also have a ripple effect on the country's politics. The state is seeing a churn in its political alignments. The decades-old BJP-Shiromani Akali Dal alliance has broken up, and ex-Congressman Captain Amarinder Singh's new party, the Punjab Lok Congress, has now entered into a tie-up with the BJP and Sukhdev Singh Dhindsa's Shiromani Akali Dal (Sanyukt). What used to, mostly, be a bipolar contest has now turned into a multi-corner fight, with the Aam Aadmi Party (AAP) emerging as a strong contender and an alternative for many. Arvind Kejriwal is holding up the Delhi model of governance, while trying to capitalize on the anti-incumbency against state government as well as the Centre.

But the event that promises to shape political trends nationally is the appointment of Charanjit Singh Channi as the state's new chief minister.

Punjab has the highest proportion of Dalits across all states in India, with nearly 32 per cent of the population belonging to Scheduled Castes. Punjab was the birthplace of Dalit leader and BSP founder Kanshi Ram. Despite this, the state has predominantly had Jat Sikhs as chief minister, till Channi became the first Dalit Sikh to ascend to the post. His appointment has even pushed the Shiromani Akali Dal and the BSP to enter into an alliance in order to lure the Dalit voter. If the Congress snatches a victory here, much of the credit would have to go to Channi and his appointment. The Congress' experiment, if successful, might also help it draw more Dalit voters towards itself nationally. Nowhere else would this be more relevant for the Grand Old Party than in Uttar Pradesh, where Mayawati's flailing campaign could see Dalits exploring other options to back. Is this 'Dalit + female voters' the secret formula that the Congress is targeting in Uttar Pradesh? Time will tell.

Uttarakhand is one state where the BJP finds itself on the defensive, after having to change three chief ministers in five years, ostensibly due to reasons of factionalism and non-performance. The AAP is trying hard to build a base there, and it remains to be seen whether the AAP can puncture the state's predominantly bipolar politics between the BJP and the Congress.

Similar is the case with Goa, where new players AAP and the TMC are looking to queer the pitch for the Congress and BJP, the predominant political powers in the state. Both parties are going all out and see the small, sunny state as an easy hunting ground to expand themselves in, with just 40 assembly seats to fight over. Despite its size, Goa has traditionally thrown up hung assemblies, and it will be interesting to see whether any of these parties agree to work with each other. That collaboration could just set a national template.

In Manipur, a resurgent BJP is likely to launch an assertive campaign to retain the state. The state was a Congress stronghold, and the party will be desperate to snatch it back from the BJP.

All these polls, from the mammoth Uttar Pradesh to the tiny Goa, have repercussions on the country's politics as it inches closer towards the 2024 polls.

Regional parties are growing increasingly assertive and are demanding a chance at leading the Opposition charge against the BJP. In many of these states, emergence of parties like the AAP and the TMC could end up dividing the anti-BJP vote and result in the BJP's victory.

That is why the results will matter a lot – a win for the Congress in at least two states will give it the confidence to assert itself and insist that it is the natural leader of any collective effort against the BJP. But if it doesn't and the BJP manages to defeat it comprehensively in all the five states, the Congress will have a lot more to ponder over. Wins for the

BJP will mean the party will walk into 2024, high on confidence.

Many of the factors that the book discusses will be at play here. For instance, the increasing voting share of female voters is a theme to watch out for, especially in Uttar Pradesh, where Gandhi Vadra is aggressively wooing this crucial demographic. The final outcome notwithstanding, this is the first time we are seeing female voters being targeted as a separate constituency by any party in Uttar Pradesh.

Similarly, Uttar Pradesh also promises to be a communally charged election. As I explain later, indulging in communalism seldom helps a party wins more votes, something that has been proven time and again by the Indian electorate.

Our team is already on the ground and is raring to go. So far, we have been on the mark in predicting forty-eight of the fifty-two elections, with an accuracy rate of 93 per cent.

I hope these five elections help it take a few percentage points higher.

Pradeep Gupta
January, 2022

Introduction: Methodology

Since 2013, out of the forty-seven exit polls conducted by Axis My India, we have hit the bullseye in forty-four. In this art of poll prediction, or science as one may call it, I cannot say what others are doing, but what we do right is put our heart and soul into it. We follow some fundamentals, which have helped us in delivering trusted solutions since 1998. The first and foremost is to 'reach' the right audience. Second, adopt the right approach to 'connect' with them, and third, make a sincere effort to 'understand' them and their needs and issues, likes and dislikes. Finally, we convince them that once we gather all information from the ground, we will collate and make sense of this data and present it to the right stakeholders, who will be able to address these issues and raise them on the right platform and this defines our vision, which is to connect and resolve the problems of the 25 crore Indian households. Axis My India's mission right from its inception has been to actively contribute every day to transforming a billion lives, and I see my job as a pollster right at the beginning of this chain which connects India to build India.

While poll predictions are a seasonal activity, Axis My India's bread and butter is our corporate business, which includes consumer insight, consumer trust index, an exhaustive exercise that runs across the country through the year and keeps us on our toes. While our same set of foot soldiers report from the ground for both the activities, poll surveys are far more rigorous, almost a military job. Considering our final output is entirely dependent on the raw data collected by the field staff and surveyors, selecting efficient and eligible team members, and training them, is key to successfully putting together the larger jigsaw puzzle in the final stages of any poll survey.

Our headhunting is an intensive exercise that covers over 700 districts in the country and is a continuous process because the attrition rate, for a variety of reasons, is high in this sector. Even if the staff does not always voluntarily choose to move on, in a number of cases we are forced to discontinue their services on account of quality issues. Out of the 700 field staff engaged in conducting surveys during the 2019 general elections, we had to send home 135 during the fieldwork after we noticed shortcomings in the accuracy level of their reporting. The slightest slip in the accuracy of data collection has a huge impact on the overall outcome, hence quality is non-negotiable.

Our massive recruitment and selection process is supported by a rigorous training system that is essential as the surveyors usually have no prior experience in the job. During the training, the focus is on explaining to them their role and approach because unless the surveyor is able to strike a chord with the interviewee/voter, candid responses will not be forthcoming. The job of the surveyor is to get an insight from the respondent, which is extremely difficult, especially when it comes to their party preference. This is because there is apprehension that the surveyor could be posing as a neutral person while belonging to a political party, and if the respondent ends up saying anything against that party, he or she could be victimized. It becomes a direct threat to their lives. So in several states where the political situation is volatile respondents are extremely cautious, and that makes our job so much tougher. Therefore, during the training process, the field staff are taught how to build trust with the respondent, how to connect with them so that they believe we are from a neutral organization and mean well.

We engage voters' interest further by offering a lucky draw or freebies on joining our survey, which also helps in developing a rapport before we get on with the actual interview. We also ensure that we hire locals who are fluent in the regional dialect and are able to converse in the same tongue. This makes a lot of difference to the quality of the engagement with the respondent. Basic grooming tips on how to dress, converse, initiate and conclude conversations are also shared. We have seen that while it is easier for male surveyors to interact with male respondents, women in rural areas are not very comfortable opening up to them. Female field staff have better access to women voters but it is not always possible to ensure a same-gender interaction, and hence male surveyors are also trained in building a rapport with women respondents to draw them out of their shell.

Like I said, the job of a surveyor is much like

a military posting, calling for great physical and mental strength. The field staff are on the ground and away from their families for fifteen days at a stretch, and travel across ten to fifteen villages every day, experiencing great hardships. Though they have an SUV to themselves and are equipped with all the facilities to ensure their mobility is not restricted, the living conditions in the remotest parts of the country are undeniably difficult. Most of our staff are from underprivileged sections of society and are therefore able to better connect with the masses owing to their shared background and life experiences. Indeed they are hardy lieutenants and exhibit far more physical and mental stamina than those from more affluent and privileged backgrounds. During the 2020 elections, our surveyors faced further hardship due to the Covid-19 pandemic. People were afraid to interact with outsiders, especially at close quarters. So we decided to use two mikes, one for the surveyor and one for the interviewee, with the cables of both mikes at three metres each so that a healthy physical distance was maintained between the two.

In every election survey, the starting point for us is to map the constituency and understand the local issues at play. These issues, along with caste and other social factors, have a great bearing on the voting pattern and preference of the voters. Once that groundwork is done, we draft a questionnaire for the pre- and post-poll surveys, taking into account demographic representative sampling of rural–urban, male–female and age ratios.

Accuracy in one's method of operation is the key to success. Throughout the data collection process, there is a great emphasis on maintaining accuracy and hence we closely monitor our surveyors end to end during the exercise on a real-time basis. When the surveyor is interviewing voters on the ground, we have a back-end team tracking the surveyor's approach, manner of questioning, quality of the conversation and accuracy of conveying the questions. If the back-end team notices any discrepancies, alerts are sent in real time, and if despite the suggested course correction the surveyor continues to be lax we take strict action. Through our GPS stamping we also get to know the exact location of the surveyor so that we are not fed fake responses.

Senior team members from the head office and regional offices and I try to join the survey teams as often as possible to get a sense of the ground realities and to keep the team members motivated. This also helps in hand-holding them through any challenges that they face on the ground and ensuring quick resolution of problems.

The fieldwork needs to be carried out with utmost attention to detail because if we slip here the next steps in the survey will fall like a pack of cards. There is absolutely no scope for error at this stage, and if a surveyor is found wanting, s/he is asked to pack up and leave. It is necessary for us to maintain a good bench strength so that in such cases we do not fall short of staff and can avoid accommodating any sort of incompetence or even mediocrity.

The surveys are done through computer-aided personal interviews (CAPI) and, apart from the GPS stamping which tracks physical movement during the interviews, real-time updates on our special tailor-made software allow a minute-by-minute tracking of the entire interview process. The software we have developed enables our back-end staff to monitor what is happening on the ground and make timely interventions so that the interviews are carried out in line with our protocols. Our back-office teams comprise competent data analysts, data scientists and political analysts who remain with us through the poll survey, and their insight into the initial and final readings are crucial in arriving at the final prediction.

We have a robust quality control system in place and to encourage accuracy we have an award and reward system based on the performance of our staff in every election. They are marked on roughly thirty parameters, such as sample collection (required versus achieved), productivity, predictive accuracy (when compared with the final results), and victory margin accuracy. These are reflected on their report cards as part of a regular appraisal cycle. To incentivize quality output and hard work, along with a hefty cash prize, their efforts are recognized through awards that are handed out by prominent sporting or Bollywood celebrities in a glitzy event at a five-star property where the entire staff is taken for a rejuvenating off-site session.

Unlike other companies involved in poll surveys, we do not hire part-timers but nurture a team over a long period. Our teams are spread across the length and breadth of the country, from Ladakh to the Andaman and Nicobar Islands. My ultimate aim is to have one team in each district, and we are working towards it. During elections, my current team of 700 field staff and 300 back-office staff are engaged in poll surveys; the rest of the year they work on other corporate or brand assignments. As for the overall organization, I have always insisted on a healthy, flat office culture, free of hierarchy, where everyone feels equal and empowered. Moreover, as we keep reminding everyone in the office, our volunteers on the ground, who conduct the interviews, are our strongest pillars in the process of poll predictions and they deserve much credit for our success.

One of our biggest challenges on the ground is that of identity. Our surveyors need to establish a credible identity before the respondents so that they are not viewed as impostors or political party workers out to gather poll-related intelligence, both of which draw extremely hostile reactions from the masses. Our surveyors have at times been stripped, tied to a tree and brutally beaten up. In West Bengal, one of the most politically sensitive states, our team members have even been sent to jail for up to ten days on false charges. Sometimes voters become suspicious of our motives and turn violent, damaging the tablets on which data is collected and locking up our surveyors in a house or taking them to the cops.

We have a legal department working round the clock to ensure that the ground staff get speedy relief but it is indeed a huge challenge to get them released from custody – a lot of strings have to be pulled. Allegations of kidnapping and other frauds are most common in these cases. For data collection by pollsters, unlike for journalists, there is no system of obtaining permission from the local authorities or a structured manner of doing this. The job comes with its share of risks and challenges and one has to work around it. So our first priority while on the ground is to establish a relationship of trust with the respondent and, as you can well imagine, to be able to do that in the very first meeting is a huge task.

While West Bengal is the worst in terms of political violence, states like Madhya Pradesh (MP), Gujarat and Maharashtra are far safer and people tend to cooperate once we succeed in convincing them that we are there to help their cause. In MP, it is also easier to communicate as mostly Hindi is spoken with minor regional variations. In metro cities, if you knock on ten doors, you end up with interviews in a maximum of three or four houses. In urban cities this could be five to six houses every ten attempts, while in rural areas eight to nine interviews are sure-shot. In urban areas there are apartments that have a closed-door system, whereas in rural areas the sense of community is strong and at any given village square you will find locals chatting away leisurely. In bigger cities like Delhi, Mumbai and Bengaluru, people have little time to spare and are also suspicious of such interactions.

Just the vast distances in this country and its climate, especially our harsh summers, add to the strain on our foot soldiers. In coastal Puri, our team was caught in the cyclone Fani that came soon after the 2019 general elections, which were held in peak summer, a particularly difficult time to reach voters across the country. There have been endless adventures while on the field which may sound like unforgettable experiences in retrospect but were times of great crises. There have been occasions, one for instance in the remote tribal area of Jhabua, Madhya Pradesh, where our team got held up till 8 p.m. and couldn't leave and so they spent the night in a local hospital, sleeping on the vacant beds there. Once one of our cabs broke down and the team had no option but to hop on to a truck to get out of that area. Once, during the general elections, a surveyor became hysterical and started crying, complaining the hotel he was staying in was haunted. From 1 a.m. to 6 a.m., he remained inconsolable and finally had to be shifted out. There have been minor accidents but, by God's grace, never any casualties. Now do you see why I call this job akin to a military posting? For me, a project is successful only once my team is back home safe because that means the final outcome will definitely be successful for us as I have tremendous faith in my team.

Thankfully, my own humble beginnings give me the mental and physical stamina to join my field force on their adventures often. As an eight-year-old in 1977, I had attended my first political rally. Of course, that adventure, just a free ride on a tempo truck, was exciting enough to get me hooked, but the fiery, impassioned political speech by a local Janata Party leader, Shri Laxmi Khandelwal, at Arambha village in the Balaghat (MP) parliamentary constituency made a very strong impression on my young mind. From then on I was fully absorbed in the world of politics, based as it is on two of my passions, human psychology and number crunching. My inherent curiosity for politics was strengthened by my father, Motilal Gupta, a freedom fighter who had worked with Mahatma Gandhi in Sevagram, Wardha. He also worked as a political adviser to leaders in Balaghat district, such as its parliamentarians and legislators, municipal presidents and councillors, before elections in Waraseoni town, and you could say I have inherited some of his skills. As a poet and writer, he dreamed that one day his son would own a printing press and media house, and to fulfil that goal he got me enrolled into a course on printing technology. Decades later, in 2013, when I went to the Harvard Business School (Boston, USA), Emeritus Professor of Leadership Development Robert S. Kaplan, former Goldman Sachs vice chairman and Federal Bank governor, told me, 'You discover what you are meant for.' When I told him that I enjoy connecting with people and understanding their issues, he was quick to suggest that I try my hand at political advisory.

In 2013, when we started poll surveys, I was transported back to a little game I played as a schoolchild. After every exam I would come home and make a quick calculation and write down what I would possibly score on the calendar. The joy of getting it right has always been overwhelming. Numbers are constantly on my mind and I absolutely love playing around with them. A calculator has the power to cure me even on my worst days. Luckily, very early on in life, I had to take charge of a full-fledged household with fourteen female members under one roof – an experience that taught me the balancing act and stood me in good stead when I went out trying to decipher what voters wanted.

Voting patterns are largely about number crunching and an insight into human psychology, how one behaves or how the human mind works in a particular situation. It is fascinating how the human mind functions differently in different situations, governed by its needs, demographics and sense of belonging. The outcome of the voter's thought process largely depends on these factors, which is why election results surprise or shock those of us who are sitting in capital cities and TV studios away from the real mood of the nation. We often mistake the sentiments of a smaller representative group accessible to us for what the larger, actual vote bank feels. And that is how we get it wrong. There is absolutely no alternative to an exhaustive ground survey, reaching out to the last voter in the boondocks.

The mantra for me clearly is: Human psychology + Sociology = Psephology.

1

Election Results Will Move in One Direction – As a Result of Technology and Communications

Indian elections have evolved a lot like Indian arranged marriages. Family or village elders, puffing on the communal hookah, no longer seal the fate of a candidate. Technology has left the ubiquitous nai (barber), who traditionally brought leads for probable matches and had a high success rate, redundant. How many parents, worried sick over their ward's insouciance, now ask their barber to find a match or run a quick background check? Hardly any. Social media snooping it is for millennials. Be it to shortlist potential alliances on a matrimonial site or to zero down on a local representative, a comparative analysis today is just a click away.

Technology has enabled voters today to share notes and build a consensus on who is 'deserving'.

Earlier, lack of communication channels kept them clueless about the views of voters in other parts of the country. Hence decision-making largely remained localized, limited to a village, town, district or at the most a state. The elderly, the socially empowered or the dominant caste/community could loosely be called 'influencers' back then, be it in an arranged marriage or an election.

Till the early 1990s, during polls we could interact only with our immediate neighbourhood – even landline phones were then a luxury. Our physical reach limited our discussions and deliberations over whom to vote for, who was a deserving candidate, the government's performance, anti-incumbency and the like. Tea-shop and nai-dukaan addas, social gatherings, lunch breaks at the workplace – opinions travelled merely by word of mouth.

The arrival of smartphones and social media has collapsed all physical boundaries and instantly connected everyone at a national and global level. In 2019, India had 373.88 million smartphone users, a sharp hike from 2017, when this figure stood at 299.24 million. According to a Comscore report, YouTube had 325 million unique monthly users in India as of May 2020. As of 2021, according to Union Minister for Communications, Electronics & Information Technology and Law & Justice Ravi Shankar Prasad, India has over 530 million WhatsApp users, over 400 million Facebook users, and over 10 million Twitter users – all essential campaign platforms for political parties.

Voters have always wanted a strong government. I see it like selecting the head of a family or a company. Unlike olden times the seniormost or eldest is now no longer the first choice. Instead, one looks for a strong and deserving successor to sort out the myriad challenges that the post-modern world has thrown up. Of course, the definition of 'deserving' is entirely relative and I am not getting into that.

On social media ideas crystallize and trend, leading to uniform opinions being formed and thumping majorities for the winner and conversely absolute negation of the loser. Whether it is positive or negative publicity, it gets communicated across the board. Opinions are shaped not only by trending ideas and raging debates on social media but also by ground realities reported from across the country. Social media has truly become a melting pot where opinions are formed in an unorganized and spontaneous manner, and quite effortlessly. Thanks to the platform that has nudged, rather awakened, the citizen journalist in each of us. Of course, some opinions are carefully crafted by political parties and I will address that shortly.

The 2014 Lok Sabha elections, the assembly elections in Delhi and Bihar in 2015, Kerala and West Bengal in 2016 and Uttar Pradesh in 2017, all gave clear, resounding majorities to a single party or an alliance. In Delhi, Arvind Kejriwal's Aam Aadmi Party (AAP) wiped out the opposition by grabbing 67 out of 70 seats in February 2015, just thirteen months after Delhi threw up a hung house. From bagging 28 seats in his electoral debut in December 2013 and a forty-nine-day stint as chief minister, Kejriwal came back as a giant in early 2015 as consensus built over the months that he could deliver if he had the numbers. This was barely eight months after the Bharatiya Janata Party (BJP) swept all seven parliamentary seats in Delhi in the 2014 general elections. The same was repeated in the 2019 parliamentary polls and the 2020 Delhi assembly elections, where again the BJP and AAP swept the state respectively.

Voters today make informed choices. They know which way the wind is blowing – the general pulse of the people is right out there. No one wants to waste their vote on a loser. This explains why the Congress party, despite Sheila Dikshit's legacy, failed to better even its voteshare in the Delhi polls. Instead, it dropped further from 9.7 per cent in 2015 to 4.2 per cent. Election after election, my interaction with voters during the pre- or post-poll surveys has convinced me that they know exactly what is on the table. The AAP that was pushed to the third spot in Delhi with 18.11 per cent vote share in the 2019 Lok Sabha polls notched up 53.57 per cent in the 2020 assembly elections, whereas the BJP that garnered 56.56 per cent in Delhi in the Lok Sabha polls managed to get only 38.51 per cent in the assembly elections. The staunchest Modi supporters, clearly, chose Kejriwal when it came to the local polls.

This has been a nationwide trend. Who doesn't want to empower a solid leader? In Kerala the Left Democratic Front bagged 91 out of 140 seats. With 325 out of 403 seats in Uttar Pradesh, the BJP remained unshakeable. The two national elections of 2014 and 2019 are proof that Indian voters no longer want precarious, wobbly governments. No more rainbow coalitions. They want a strong leader and a solid majority that will push through definitive legislation. The BJP has powered through a slew of pro-poor schemes like the Ujjwala Yojana (free gas connection), Ayushman Bharat (health insurance worth Rs 5 lakh), Jan Dhan Yojana (zero balance bank account opening), soil testing for farmers, Swachh Bharat Mission and Mudra Yojana since 2014, which has lent Modi the image of an effective administrator. The fun part is political parties have been able to widen their reach manyfold without their campaign budgets seeing a proportionate increase thanks to cost-effective technological tools. Back in the 1970s and 1980s, leaders, even the most hard-working of them, be it Indira Gandhi or Atal Bihari Vajpayee, could manage to pack in only a few rallies per day. Their audience remained only those they could reach and address physically. Leaders roughly managed five rallies or so a day even if they pushed themselves really hard at the hustings and the next day only a fraction of the population read about it in the newspapers. Today every rally is telecast live on the social media handles of the respective political parties, instantly expanding the leader's and the party's reach. Every speech recording is heard several times over and circulated through WhatsApp even long after it is delivered. In terms of physical reach too, multiple LED screens inside and sometimes outside the venue help pack in larger crowds at a single event. Sometimes they are livestreamed across cities and towns, widening the targeted audience manyfold.

Technology has thrown up interesting challenges for the Election Commission in the meantime. Political parties have found convenient ways to flout the model code of conduct that imposes restrictions on campaigning 48 hours before polling. Even as campaigning comes to a halt in a poll-bound state or constituency ahead of polling day, leaders move on to other constituencies and the campaign continues streaming live on everyone's smartphone. Technically campaigning goes on till the last vote of the day is cast. Leaders usually get on with their campaigns in constituencies or states where there are no such restrictions as elections are a few days or weeks away, killing two birds with one stone.

On a relaxed Sunday morning, 19 May 2019, as Prime Minister Narendra Modi sat meditating in a flowing saffron robe, with the snowclad Himalaya in the backdrop, his every move livestreaming on news channels, voters across 59 constituencies trooped to polling booths to cast their votes. It was the seventh and final phase of voting, one that would be a direct verdict on Modi's governance. Large parts of key states like West Bengal, Madhya Pradesh, Uttar Pradesh, Punjab, Bihar and Himachal Pradesh were deciding whether Modi deserved another chance. All this while the prime minister's brief detox at a 15-hour meditation session in a Kedarnath cave – what was termed as the first break in his five years of all-work-and-no-play stint – unfolded as a soft campaign that only advertising professionals can read into. Maybe others should take a page from such strategies, because you are playing to win after all. Though the Election Commission has laid down social media guidelines and is constantly working to plug all loopholes, politicians continue to get the better of them.

Effectively, communication has flowed in two ways – leader to voter and voter to voter – and both ways have led to informal opinion formulation. Social media has blurred the boundaries for leaders. Politicians have always been held accountable for their utterances, scrutinized for their comments that go into an indelible archive. In the age of social media, perceptions are created against political opponents without so much as a thought given to propriety. Leaders earlier did not have the privilege of this anonymity if they wished to run a full-fledged slander campaign against their political adversaries. In the pre-social-media era, leaders could not afford to go wrong with their communication strategy. There was no Twitter to turn to the next day, no follow-up comments could be made, no real-time feedback of the previous speech was available for the leader to make corrections soon after.

Today allegations are hurled without any attribution to authentic sources. In many cases, the politician's public relations machinery does it for him. Surrogate pages on Facebook, Twitter, Instagram and WhatsApp forwards are all tools that every political party employs ruthlessly to build its own campaign and demolish its opponent's. Who exactly came up with 'Pappu' for Rahul Gandhi for the first time? Perhaps we will never know, but its originating source we all know only too well. This casual, spontaneous springboarding of monikers by one political party against its opponents helps it land on a premise that has already clicked with a large vote base. When a public image is being built or broken it depends on whether the propagator or the defender has a stronger social media team. While the 'Pappu' tag has haunted Rahul Gandhi for a good part of his political career, the Congress party's counter for Narendra Modi, 'suit boot ki sarkar', referring to his pricey hologram suit, did not stick for too long because Modi was quick to take remedial action. Some names stick, some don't. The question of their ingenuity is another story for another day.

Voter turnout has progressively increased and the consolidation of ideas on social media has translated into landslide victories. More people thinking alike also means more people making the same choices. Voting figures in the past three decades have gone up ten percentage points, from hovering at 57–58 per cent in the 1990s to 67.4 per cent in 2019. Today even as rural–urban migration has displaced a sizeable section of the voting population, voters are only a call away. While the Election Commission through its publicity has pushed voters to come out of their houses to cast their ballot, candidates leave no stone unturned to ensure their supporters travel back home during elections to vote for them. Technology has spared no one, not even a reluctant voter.

It has, however, positively ensured better monitoring, accuracy and faster counting of votes and safekeeping of the electronic voting machines in

CCTV-monitored strongrooms. Gone are the days of booth capturing that possibly at a hyperlocal level upset what could have been a larger national trend. Something we can retrospectively only speculate, never know for sure.

Add to this the gradual demographic shift to a larger younger population that is impacted by social media and technology advancement. If in 2001 there were 21 crore eligible voters in the age group of eighteen to twenty-nine years, in 2019 this figure went up to 30 crore. Voters in the age group of thirty to thirty-nine years increased from 14 crore in 2001 to 22 crore in 2019. The percentage of young voters has seen a steady rise, displacing old preferences in terms of candidates and political parties and outmoded campaign tools and techniques. So we have more young voters who are out there sharing ideas on social media, evaluating them, propagating them, influencing their contemporaries and sometimes even the older generation, arriving largely at a consensus and delivering thumping majorities.

Social media and 24x7 news channels have invaded the privacy of politicians, putting the spotlight on infighting, blame games and tussles for power within political parties that also end up hurting their own prospects. Social media and 24x7 news channels keep a hawk's eye on the goings-on in a politician's life, relaying the nitty-gritties to an ever-inquisitive audience. Take the Punjab elections in 2017, for instance. The AAP that appeared poised to get 100 out of the 117 seats ended up with just 20 due to the bitter internal tussle in the party that played out in front of a national audience. The Congress made unexpected gains in the four months leading to the polls, and a dormant Captain Amarinder Singh emerged stronger than ever before with 77 seats in his kitty.

In Uttar Pradesh, the infighting in the Samajwadi Party cost them heavily while the BJP that was trailing in the second position in all pre-poll surveys leapt ahead at the last minute, grabbing over 80 per cent of the seats in the assembly. Both these elections gave clear, sweeping verdicts.

That is not to say that the village elders or dominant castes have lost their sway over their communities, especially in north India. When our survey teams hit the ground, they are invariably told that a final call on which party to back will be taken once the community meetings are held. Jats, Muslims and Dalits across the country exhibit the strongest sense of community when they vote. Communication has come as a boon for them, ensuring homogeneity in their opinion formulation and voting preferences. Earlier fatwas were issued through maulvis to consolidate the Muslim vote but now smartphones have connected everyone. Victory or loss in most elections is decisive.

For instance, khaps in Haryana have a very strong network. They consult among themselves and issue a diktat right before the polls. Earlier the talks would be held over a mahapanchayat, but now the consensus-building starts much earlier, as khaps reach out to one another over the phone, weigh their options and begin building public sentiment, 'mahaul', for the candidate and party of their choice. In the 2019 Haryana polls, out of 32 Jat-dominated seats, candidates in 24 seats won by a margin of over 10,000 votes, a clear indication that Jat voters made clear choices in favour of a single party despite several Jat candidates in the fray. Interestingly, most seats were bagged either by the Congress or the Jannayak Janata Party (JJP), both led by strong Jat leaders, Bhupinder Singh Hooda and Dushyant Chautala respectively. On all these seats, the BJP remained in the second spot, in a clear indication that the Jat vote did not get split between the Congress and the JJP. The BJP led by Manohar Lal Khattar, a non-Jat, managed to grab just 7 of the 32 seats. In what would otherwise have been a confusing election, with the JJP, the Indian National Lok Dal (INLD) and Congress all wooing the same community, voters smartly sifted the best options for themselves on a seat-by-seat basis. They ruled out the INLD and chose the Congress or JJP with extreme clarity. I attribute this maturity solely to a good communication network.

Conversely, in the Lok Sabha elections in 2014 in Mahasamand in Chhattisgarh, local heavyweight and former chief minister Ajit Jogi's strategy to spread misinformation against his contender helped him narrow down the margin. The BJP's Chandu Lal Sahu, who was expected to win by virtue of the 'tsunamo' (landslide victory credited to Modi), ended up getting past the line by a thin margin of 1600 votes as his opponents propped up ten namesakes. The other Chandu Lal Sahus ate into the BJP contender's votes, giving Jogi the edge.

A hilarious story, from 2003, in Madhya Pradesh comes to mind. In Paraswada constituency, political adversaries of the local heavyweight, Kankar Munjare of the Samajwadi Party, ganged up and fielded a local tribal, Darboosingh Uikey, against him. Uikey was funded and fuelled to take on Munjare and, in an unexpected turn of events, he ended up defeating Munjare. Uikey, the ragged, barefoot pawn, was so petrified after his victory that he went missing and the divisional magistrate was then tasked to hunt him down. Uikey was dragged back to acknowledge his victory. Poor communication and lack of technology cost some big leaders big heartbreaks for no fault of their own.

2

Delivery, Delivery, Delivery

Unlike most relationships in life, the one between a government and its voters is fairly uncomplicated. It is unabashedly transactional. If an elected political party or leader delivers on the promises made, people do not usually disappoint them. It is a symbiotic relationship in that sense. Each time I reach out to voters ahead of or during an election, I am increasingly convinced that several other factors that a discerning media and political pundits attribute electoral wins and losses to are merely theoretical and anecdotal. Political ideology, communalism, the lack of a strong opposition contender or the charisma of a single leader rarely factor, and if they do they are much lower in the list of priorities, for the average Indian voter. In any political party's campaign, the voter has just one main expectation – what is in it for me?

It is essential to define the average Indian voter here. As we know, anyone above the age of 18 years is eligible to cast their vote and is part of the electorate. Of this vast population of voters, 80 per cent are from rural parts of the country and/or are poor while the remaining are from urban areas and/or are well off. Those who come under the administrative units of gram or nagar panchayats, that is, roughly 6,00,000 villages, and/or have a monthly income of less than Rs 10,000 are considered rural/poor. The remaining voters who are governed by nagar palikas (municipalities) or nagar nigams (municipal corporations), roughly over 6000 in all, are counted as urban. While not everyone in the rural areas can be called poor, not everyone living in big cities have a monthly income of more than Rs 10,000.

Based on existing statistics, we can safely say that 80 per cent of the people who turn up to cast their votes are rural and poor voters. This vote bank primarily calls the shots and is the one that all political parties pander to. They are heavily dependent on the government's social security schemes and for them the government is one of the major sources of income, their 'mai-baap'. Through a slew of measures such as pension schemes, healthcare benefits, unemployment assistance, farm loan waivers, minimum support prices (MSPs), subsidies on essential commodities and monthly rations, the government either supplements and enhances their income or minimizes their expenses. So for this section of society, every election counts because they have to live with the consequences of their choices for the next five years. They never lose sight of what they expect from the government and hence inconsequential things like temple politics or minority appeasement are never uppermost on their minds. That does not put food on their table.

More than the promises made by the opposition or the challenger to the incumbent, voters evaluate the delivery of promises made by the incumbent in his/her tenure. The parameters are many, but the basics include eight specific areas – roads, electricity, water, health, education, law and order, farmer-related issues and inflation. All of these directly affect the lives and livelihoods of the 80 per cent population that usually decides where an election is headed. For the remaining 20 per cent only a few of these factors really count. The rich urban voter has nothing to do with government schools or hospitals. Farmers' issues do not affect them either. Their generator sets and power backup systems and water storage and filtration systems leave little dependence on the government unless the latter really goofs up. Law and order, the state of roads and inflation are the only three areas that have a direct impact on the lives of the rich, even if not as much as they do on the underprivileged.

Different issues take precedence at different levels of governance. In a municipal poll, subjects like drainage, garbage collection, condition of roads, drinking water supply, beautification of the city like gardens, parks, playgrounds, arrangements for cultural activities, celebration of festivals (for example Chhatt in Delhi, Ganesh Chaturthi in Maharashtra) and visibility of the councillor are deciding factors for the voter. At the assembly level, what matters are health infrastructure, government schools and colleges, public distribution system, drinking water supply, electricity, employment opportunities, roads, law and order, state-level taxes and farmer-related issues. However, voters prioritize these issues differently in different states. While law and order might be a big concern for voters in Uttar

Pradesh, it has very little significance for those in Madhya Pradesh. At the national level, larger issues that impact policymaking, such as the state of the economy, banking regulations, announcement and implementation of schemes for different sections of society (poor, farmers, labour), national security, foreign policy, infrastructure for business, air and rail travel and taxation are at play.

For the rural voter, the expectations from the government are higher. The delivery, or lack thereof, of social welfare schemes like the Mahatma Gandhi National Rural Employment Guarantee Scheme (MGNREGS), MSP, relief packages during droughts, floods, unseasonal rain and hailstorms that ravage crops, etc., play a huge role in deciding the fate of an incumbent. In 2017, when a bumper crop of onions in Madhya Pradesh led to losses for the farmers who did not know what to do with them, then chief minister Shivraj Singh Chouhan deposited hundreds of crores into their accounts under two schemes – Mukhya Mantri Kisan Bhavantar Yojana and Mukhya Mantri Krishak Samriddhi Yojana – bailing them out when the mandi prices fell below the MSP. It was unheard of that the government would buy and store onions that would be an additional expense on the exchequer. This among other pro-poor, pro-farmer schemes has seen Chouhan consolidate his position in the state, and even when he lost to Kamal Nath in December 2018, the margin was so thin that the Congress government toppled within 15 months flat. Similarly, the landslide verdict in favour of the Congress party in Chhattisgarh in 2018 was based on its pre-poll promise of higher MSP for paddy and farm loan waivers. Whereas in the last two elections, the difference in the vote share of the BJP and Congress was 0.4 per cent and 0.6 per cent respectively, in 2018 this widened to 10 per cent. Our surveys found that the Congress party's promise of Rs 2200 as MSP for paddy as against the existing rate of Rs 1700 under Raman Singh won the farmers over. The rice bowl of India couldn't resist this temptation and the timing of the announcement couldn't have been any better. It was just before Diwali when the farmer was harvesting his fields that the Congress brought them the good news. Barely fifteen days before the first phase of elections, winds of change began to sweep the state and our surveyors came back with reports that the Congress was on the surge, riding high on massive farmer backing. Incumbent chief minister Raman Singh, despite a clean and good public image even after three consecutive terms, lost to the hopes that the Congress successfully managed to sell. During our surveys, when we asked the voters what if the Congress did not keep its word, they told us, 'Agli election mein dekhlenge' (We will fix it in the next election). And so they did. Four months later, in the parliamentary polls in 2019, the BJP swept the state. Of course there are several factors at play here. The extremely short window of delivery for the state government could not bring a turnaround for the Congress in the national elections. Also the voter today is extremely mature and sharp-witted. He knows exactly who to vote for in which election. They got what they wanted from the state government and now in the general elections it was a verdict on Prime Minister Modi's delivery of promises like gas connections, toilets and housing for all, to name a few.

The verdict in Delhi in February 2020 too backs my theory. Despite some of the brightest candidates in the fray, who had absolute clean track records and were promising young faces, the AAP lost the 2019 parliamentary polls, demoted to the third spot on most seats. Party supremo Arvind Kejriwal's strong governance failed to convince the voter that the AAP deserved better representation in Parliament. Less than nine months after sweeping all seven seats in the national capital in the parliamentary polls, the BJP had to make do with just 8 out of 70 seats in the assembly polls. Amid a highly polarized campaign that led several pollsters to either sit on the fence or give AAP a marginal win, we at Axis My India were the only ones to stick our necks out for a landslide victory of AAP. Braving Delhi's brutal cold, in those smog-filled mornings, when I spoke at length with respondents – tea-stall owners, rickshaw pullers, drivers, hawkers, random pedestrians – they all told me in one voice that Kejriwal had looked after them well. They were extremely grateful for the free bijli–paani, the revamped government schools where their children went and the mohalla clinics that were at least there even if not always well stocked. The women were happy with their free bus rides. There are always some deficiencies in the implementation of government schemes, but the voter is forgiving and non-judgemental as long as s/he is convinced that the person in power genuinely cares.

I must confess I was a little nervous before the results came out. The BJP's confidence till the very last minute and the predictions of the other pollsters threw me into serious self-doubt. I am glad we stuck to our basics in our survey – reading the voter right.

I have often been intrigued by the politics of the Biju Janata Dal (BJD) chief and five-time Odisha chief minister, Naveen Patnaik. He barely has any visibility in the media, no self-obsessive appearances on television advertisements or hoardings, no social media gimmicks, he is not the most fluent Odiya speaker, nor are his oratory skills outstanding. Though he is never out of touch with his people, he is also never seen in office after 6 p.m. working overtime. Unlike the BJP, his party cannot boast of a strong organization. Yet one of the poorest states of the country repeatedly reposes its faith in him. While he has no family baggage to pull him down and no dynasts to tarnish his clean image, Naveen Babu's single-minded focus on delivery of services has turned him into the messiah of the people. The Odisha assembly polls always coincide with the general elections but, despite a Modi wave sweeping the country, the voter in Odisha never loses sight of what their chief minister has done for them. In fact, even in the parliamentary polls, though the BJP made significant gains in 2019 going up from a single seat in 2014 to 8 in 2019, the BJD continued to maintain its lead even there. It is Naveen Babu's strong delivery of the basic essentials that is blocking the BJP from sweeping the state.

A leader essentially has to address the grievances of the people and deliver what is within his means. For a local elected representative is expected to be available and visible in his constituency, the chief minister or prime minister is expected to be seen making a difference to the lives of the people. Passionate speeches and moving oratory are all too well till delivery takes a back seat. For the 'janta', that is unpardonable and the sole cause for a party or leader's downfall. Like Subhas Bose had said, 'No real change in history has ever been achieved by discussions.' You need action. And that is what unassailable leaders like Modi, Naveen Patnaik, Arvind Kejriwal and Nitish Kumar are delivering. In 2016, Jayalalithaa became the first chief minister in Tamil Nadu since M.G. Ramachandran to be re-elected, thanks to her welfare schemes. Women and the marginalized sections voted heavily in her favour.

When for the first four years of his second term Kejriwal kept locking horns with Modi and accusing him of putting a spanner in his works, he consecutively lost elections. The mandate was not for Kejriwal to point out the limitations of his jurisdiction and power but for him to deliver within the constraints of the constitution. Like three-time Congress chief minister Sheila Dikshit did. Ahead of the 2020 assembly elections, Kejriwal went back to the drawing board and expedited schemes that were under his government and he remained non-confrontational. People do not expect leaders to deliver what is not within their means. Their expectations are realistic. A leader only has to be a fair and strict administrator and do the right thing by his people. That is all that matters. And that is why Modi is such a rage today.

While Modi's delivery in his first term got him a bigger mandate in 2019, the Congress party was very close to upsetting the apple cart. After winning three state elections in Rajasthan, Madhya Pradesh and Chhattisgarh in December 2018, the Congress party was on a high. They seemed to have finally got the pulse of the people and their NYAY scheme (Nyunatam Aay – minimum income guarantee) had sent the BJP into a tizzy. In the first week of the launch of this poll promise, two newspaper advertisements went with a catchy tagline – Abki baar 72,000. People had begun to get hooked when the slogan changed to 'Ab hoga NYAY', which translated to 'Now there will be justice'. In the backdrop of this campaign, the party went hammer and tongs after Modi and the alleged Rafale scam. Voters soon lost interest. In our surveys, we specifically asked them if they knew about NYAY and, if yes, what exactly it was. Less than 20 per cent of the electorate were aware of the proposed scheme and even if they had heard about it they confused it with 'delivery of justice' against the Rafale scam. Communication has a journey and even if we wish to blend in with the abbreviation-savvy millennial, we should spare a thought for the dominant electorate that cares little for such fads. The poor, rural voter means business and it is best to speak to them in a tongue they comprehend.

There is a reason the masses do not hold it against Modi for not depositing Rs 15 lakh in their accounts. Voters knew it was a euphemism for bringing back black money and even if Modi did not have anything concrete to show for it his demonetization gambit pretty much made up for it all. The poor, rural voters felt they had little to lose in this while they saw the rich scramble to save their stashed moolah. Promises made by political leaders are always taken with a pinch of salt but if the voter goes to bed hungry then you have most certainly turned her against you.

3

Women Emerging as an Important Vote Bank

'I've learned that people will forget what you said, people will forget what you did, but people will never forget how you made them feel.'

– Maya Angelou

Since the beginning of civilization, women have kept households running by making prudent choices between needs and wants. In twenty-first-century India, their increasing participation in the workforce and independent decision-making due to financial self-sufficiency and women's liberation have led to a marked rise in women exercising their franchise – from 53.6 per cent women voter turnout in 2004 to 67.2 per cent in 2019 – and political parties have been rather quick on the uptake.

In addition to minority appeasement, pro-poor and caste politics, politicians are discovering a brand-new vote bank that is helping them sail through elections – the woman voter. My reading of the several state and national elections over the past decade is that there is an unmistakable emerging trend – the unshakeable leaders almost always enjoy the overwhelming support of women voters. Be it Prime Minister Narendra Modi or chief ministers M.G. Ramachandran, Arvind Kejriwal, Naveen Patnaik or J. Jayalalithaa, they have especially watched out for the women in their care and received all the love and votes in reciprocation. Bihar Chief Minister Nitish Kumar too appealed to this vote bank and caught the popular imagination by his 'sushasan babu' image. The prohibition of alcohol under his last regime and distribution of cycles to girl students have been hugely popular with the women electorate.

While sops and schemes for women have taken up a key section in the election manifestos that are now distinctly segmented for their target audiences, leaders tirelessly pander to the 'mataon, behnon aur betiyon' (mothers, sisters and daughters) of the nation, knowing full well that they hold the key to their fortunes. Modi's second term in office is largely thanks to delivery of promises made in 2014. There were three very successful schemes that proved to be the game changer in 2019 – free gas connections (Ujjwala), toilets (Swachh Bharat) and housing for all (PM Awas Yojana) – and all of them had the woman voter at the centre of their marketing strategy. Modi talked of giving women the luxury of smokeless kitchens and the dignity of a private toilet and pandered to the 'grihalakshmi' in them through his pet projects. All Modi had to do was rename the Indira Awas Yojana, deliver it right and publicize it well among his target audience, and there he had the perfect formula to win hearts. These remained the central theme of his rallies since he came to power in 2014, and my surveys ahead of the 2019 general elections clearly indicate that the resounding mandate he got was based largely on these. The Modi government's audacious legislation criminalizing triple talaq following the Supreme Court's verdict abolishing the regressive practice was yet another move to woo women from a community that has traditionally been wary of the BJP.

Delhi Chief Minister Arvind Kejriwal, who won his third consecutive election in 2020, offered a slew of freebies targeted at women. He introduced free bus and metro rides for women and spoke of ways to ramp up women's security through better street lights, CCTV cameras and marshals in public buses. The makeover of government schools with parent–teacher meetings, summer camps, English-speaking classes and swanky campuses left the mothers highly impressed while free water and power made him their messiah. Like Modi, Kejriwal had zeroed in on his audience well in advance and through his campaign referred to himself as 'aapka bada bhai' or 'ghar ka bada beta'. For a government to come back with such a clean sweep is a clear verdict of its popularity, and this happened because women threw their weight behind him.

Unlike minority or caste-based voting patterns, there is no homogeneity in the voting trends of women. It will be highly inaccurate if I were to say that women across the country went out to vote making their own independent choices. But I will take the liberty of making another rather simplistic yet factual observation. If women voters were to be classified according to region, I would say women in the five southern states of Kerala, Tamil Nadu, Karnataka, Andhra Pradesh and Telangana vote independently sans the influence of male members of the family whereas in north India (if we were to consider the rest of the country) they go by the judgement of the dominant male in the household, usually the father, husband or father-in-law. Our interaction with women voters during surveys in a state like Rajasthan is very limited. This is true for all of north India where the practice of purdah or ghunghat is prevalent compared to the south where women are far more chatty and well informed.

The link between literacy levels and financial independence with independent decision-making is undeniable. Literacy decides profession, which in turn decides a woman's financial status and independence of thought. If you are a working woman and if you contribute to the cumulative household income, your preferences begin to count and you become a part of the decision-making in the small and big things at stake.

As we all know, literacy rates in the southern states are way higher than in the rest of the country. This is true of the percentage of women in the active workforce too. But the nature of the job is not always as important as her financial independence. Literacy, however, means more informed choices and awareness of one's rights. I couldn't help but make this distinction between the voting patterns of women in southern India and the rest of the country after it got me into serious trouble once. And that is a story I cannot not share as it was one of the rare occasions I went wrong with my poll prediction – all because I ignored this important vote bank.

I wouldn't say we were lazy but that we extrapolated our experiences in the rest of the country, where men decide voting preferences for the entire family, to the voting patterns of women in Tamil Nadu. I am not making a casual, generic statement here and I hope I won't draw the ire of the very many strong, well-informed and educated women in the northern, eastern and western regions of the country. I am simply citing voting trends. In these three regions, particularly in Rajasthan, Uttar Pradesh, Punjab, Haryana, Maharashtra, Gujarat, West Bengal and Odisha, our surveyors are told by women voters, primarily rural, that they will decide after speaking to the head of the family, who is always a male member. In most cases, they are too shy to even have a freewheeling conversation, and if they did confide in us and told us what they liked or disliked about a leader or the incumbent government, they mostly would not talk decisively of their choice of political party or candidate. Very often, they would say, 'Aap unse baat kar lijiye, woh jo kahenge. [You speak to him, whatever he decides.]' We observed that whatever the men told us about their voting preference, the outcome or verdict was in line with it.

The Tamil Nadu story was an eye-opener of sorts and has been a major learning curve for me personally. In the summer of 2016, our surveyors were fanned out across the state and hard at work. It was a single-phase election, which meant less reaction time as we had to report exit polls the same day. Since the exit polls go on air by 6.30 p.m. as soon as voting concludes, we had to wrap up our survey by 4 p.m. and collate and crunch data as the clock ticked. We were using the archaic pen and paper technique during our survey, and due to paucity of time we did not manage to cover female respondents in proportion to their voting percentage. Of course, the data collection took time because of the manual entry process and slowed us down further.

Axis My India predicted a win for DMK+, that is, the Dravida Munnetra Kazhagam–led coalition, with 124–140 seats out of the 232 seats on which polls were held (two seats were left out), with the All India Anna Dravida Munnetra Kazhagam (AIADMK) trailing at 89–101. The result, much to my chagrin, was the opposite. The AIADMK won 135 seats while the DMK got 96. The margin of victory between the AIADMK and DMK+Congress was only 1.03 per cent, so it was a close contest, but I want to tell you exactly where we went wrong. I took a hard look at our survey techniques before going back to the drawing board. In our exit poll, 88 per cent of the respondents were male and only 12 per cent were female. It was grossly skewed towards men and in our post-result analysis we found that the female voters differed from the men in their choices. When we broke down the voting preferences shared with us in the survey, it was right there before us. Of the total male voters we surveyed, 36 per cent said they would vote for the AIADMK, 41 per cent chose the DMK, 10 per cent were for the Desiya Mupokku Dravida Kazhagam (DMDK) and the Congress and the BJP had 2 per cent each. Women openly backed Amma, J. Jayalalithaa. About 47 per cent women chose the AIADMK, 36 per cent went with the DMK, 8 per cent were for the DMDK, 2 per cent backed the BJP and 1 per cent were for the Congress. We were so close yet so far. While the responses were in line with the final results, our sample profile was all wrong. Not only did we switch to a more scientific data collection system through CAPIs on tablets for error-free and real-time data availability, we also started taking the opinion of women voters in this part of the country far more seriously.

Jayalalithaa held a special place in the hearts of women. Our surveyors later told me how the women were staunch believers in Amma and were convinced that everything they owned, from home appliances to saris, was given to them by her. The men, however, felt a tad neglected and were hoping to bring 'Kalaignar' M. Karunanidhi back to power. Evidently the women had their way.

To her supporters, Jayalalithaa, 'despite being a woman', was an authoritative personality. She had doled out household and kitchen appliances and utility products such as pressure cookers, gas stoves, fridges, television sets, utensils, saris, bindis and shringar kits. Even matchboxes and lighters were branded with her party symbol, two leaves. She connected with the women in the state like no one could. Though Tamil Nadu did not see stable governments, Amma was larger than life. She was wise in having known the position of women in south Indian households and not neglecting this important vote base.

However, not all women leaders are seen as champions of the female electorate. West Bengal Chief Minister and Trinamool Congress supremo Mamata Banerjee is popular for taking on the Left following years of misrule, while the Bahujan Samaj Party chief Mayawati is considered a Dalit mascot.

Our experience in the recent Bihar assembly polls was similar to Tamil Nadu in 2016. This time though we did not repeat the mistake of neglecting the crucial female vote bank, we failed to make an accurate prediction since the exact voter turnout for male and female voters was not available until two days after the exit polls were announced. The overall female voter turnout was 5.13 per cent more than the male percentage, which was revealed to us much after the exit polls were aired. This female vote share was heavily in favour of the BJP–Janata Dal (United) (JD[U]) combine. In the first phase of voting, in which men marginally voted more than women, a difference of 2.47 per cent, our predictions were more or less in line with the results. We had predicted 50 seats for the Mahagathbandhan and they bagged 47, while we expected the BJP–JD(U) combine to get 16 seats but they won 22. The second and third phases had a higher difference in the male and female voter turnouts – 6.29 per cent and 10.64 per cent more women than men voted in the second and third phases respectively. Had these figures been announced earlier, our calculations might have been more accurate. To add to this, Covid-19 restrictions limited our number of women voter interviews. Unfortunately, this was the third time in my career as a psephologist that I was way off the mark.

In a marked difference from north Indian households, women in the south often confided in our surveyors and asked them not to tell the husband about their choice of party or candidate. We often came out of a house with two diametrically opposite views. In the north, that is unthinkable.

In my view, the rise in overall literacy rates in the country is inextricably linked to increase in voter turnout. From 59.99 per cent in 1999, we moved to 67.4 per cent in 2019 as educated and aware voters want to make every vote count. The literacy rate among women on a national average is 65.46 per cent as against 80 per cent among men but the southern states fare much better than the north. According to Census 2011, literacy rates of women in Kerala (92.1 per cent), Tamil Nadu (73.4 per cent) and Karnataka (68.1 per cent) are significantly higher than those in Uttar Pradesh (57.2 per cent), Madhya Pradesh (59.2 per cent), Rajasthan (52.1 per cent) and Bihar (51.5 per cent). Punjab (70.7 per cent) and Maharashtra (75.9 per cent) are exceptions here, but literacy rates are not directly proportional to women's workforce participation and hence cannot be the sole measure of their independence. Cultural traditions and societal norms heavily dictate the position of women. Despite reasonably high rates of literacy, only 13.91 per cent women in Punjab are part of the combined rural and urban workforce while in Kerala it is just 18 per cent. In that respect, women in Andhra Pradesh (36.16 per cent), Karnataka (31.87 per cent) and Tamil Nadu (31.8 per cent) are better off in terms of their workforce participation.

While the female voter is being wooed like never before, political parties are yet to give them the agency they deserve. The Women's Reservation Bill proposing to grant 33 per cent reserved seats to women in the Lok Sabha and all state legislative assemblies remains a distant dream. While women appeasement is all very good, men in politics seem reluctant to share the space equally with women, rather like the erstwhile powerful royal families, where patriarchy was dominant.

How many women presidents can a superpower like the United States boast of? Telling, isn't it? Can men alone contribute to nation-building? Will that be a wholesome society? There is only one right answer to that. No!

4

Communalism

While every India–Pakistan cricket match unites the entire nation, in our victory and loss alike, it is ironical how the collective memory of the wounds of Partition stands to divide us as a people. I have a clear observation of polling trends and I hope political leaders reading will note – polarization can never be the main reason for your victory.

That may sound like a rather sweeping statement to make but I will argue my case patiently. Since the first poll prediction I made in 2013, I have repeatedly asked voters what counts in an election and I can tell you with some certainty I have never come across anyone who has prioritized temple construction or minority appeasement when they choose their representatives. That is not to say that communities do not have their sympathies with a particular political party with a certain ideology that is in line with their own religious beliefs. Political parties will always continue to enjoy their traditional support base even as they make their best efforts to invade and engage their rival's vote bank.

Polarization typically works when the incumbent has a solid report card while the challenger is at a loss and does not have much to show in terms of fresh promises or is unable to demolish the incumbent's claims. Since the incumbent is always evaluated on the basis of the outgoing government's or individual's performance, the challenger's only opportunity is to highlight the failures and punch holes in the incumbent's claims. Only when this does not pan out as per expectations does the challenger resort to a slander campaign or make a polarization bid to consolidate votes from a single community. The examples are far too many and the most recent reminder was the Delhi assembly polls in February 2020. The nationwide unrest following the abrogation of Article 370, the Citizenship Amendment Act (CAA) and the proposed National Register of Citizens (NRC) in the winter of 2019 made for the perfect recipe for a highly polarized poll battle two months later. The protest at Shaheen Bagh against the exclusion of Muslims from the Citizenship Amendment Act kept the pot boiling while hate speeches by local leaders added fuel to fire. Incumbent Delhi chief minister Arvind Kejriwal, fully aware of the pitfalls of letting the campaign derail by falling into the communal trap, repeatedly harped on how he would talk of nothing but his government's performance. He dodged questions on Shaheen Bagh, refused to openly woo the minorities, and till the time the model code of conduct kicked in he kept churning out pro-people policies. As this went hugely in his favour, the opposition BJP in a desperate bid escalated its 'nationalism' card. Their leaders crossed the line so many times that the Election Commission had to repeatedly intervene and issue a ban on campaigning on a few of them. The countdown to the results gave me sleepless nights probably as much as those in the contest. Despite the BJP's confidence of a sure-shot victory, my predictions stood vindicated as the AAP swept the assembly with 62 out of 70 seats, just 5 seats short of their previous tally. For an incumbent government that is a stellar performance.

Now had the AAP not been able to deliver, the

opposition's campaign would have worked like a dream because it would have added to the existing anger of the voters. Instead, the BJP's campaign backfired as it appeared like a diversionary tactic by the opposition, particularly at a time Kejriwal stuck to his script and came out with his 'Lage raho Kejriwal' slogan that drove home his message of good governance.

Even as I keep insisting that 'delivery' is the key to success, I will tread cautiously and acknowledge that in some cases a highly polarized poll battle does affect approximately 10 per cent of the seats won. While I would credit Modi's resounding victory in 2019 almost entirely to his delivery of promises in the first term, the campaign around the Balakot strikes, the slew of patriotic commercial movies like *Uri* and others on his initiatives like *Toilet: Ek Prem Katha* contributed significantly to image-building. 'Nationalism', 'deshbhakt', 'go to Pakistan' became a part of our lexicon like never before. To entirely dismiss that would be an unpardonable oversight but to give it more weightage than the Modi government's good governance will be a far bigger folly.

A large section of society, including intellectuals and the media, has often attributed Modi's smooth sailing at the hustings to the support of his party's ideological parent, the Rashtriya Swayamsevak Sangh (RSS). But I beg to differ. Had that been the case, how did the BJP fail to do well in the Lok Sabha polls following the Babri Masjid demolition when the country clearly seemed far more polarized. In 1996 the BJP won 161 seats; in 1998 and again in 1999 it managed to emerge as the single largest party with 182 seats both times. While Ram Mandir remained the centrepiece of the BJP's manifesto each time, its campaigns were more rounded and spoke as much of development. In 2014, the BJP recorded its first big victory on a pro-development and anti-corruption poll plank. At the end of the United Progressive Alliance's second term, Modi played up the corruption charges against the Manmohan Singh government while projecting Gujarat as the development model. Ramjanmabhoomi and Hindu rashtra were nowhere on its top agenda though the RSS worked silently behind the scenes keeping its cadre motivated with those promises. The mainstream voter, however, chose the promise of a corruption-free India and a new dawn. The dedicated foot soldiers of the RSS deserve all the credit as they form the crucial backbone of the BJP's campaign on the ground, taking its message to the farthest corners of the country, knocking door to door from Jammu and Kashmir to the North-East. But its ideology barely played a role in winning the hearts of the voters. Modi's public image and the BJP's campaign strategy in 2014 remained the game changers.

If communalism did pivot poll fortunes, how is it that the BJP remained on the fringes while the Samajwadi Party and the Bahujan Samaj Party dominated the Uttar Pradesh legislative assembly for decades? An inherently right-wing party in that case should have always caught the imagination of its vote bank and never conceded any of it to its rivals.

In the parliamentary polls, the BJP increased its seat share in West Bengal remarkably from 2 in 2014 to 18 in 2019 because people began seeing it as their next best option. People have already given Trinamool Congress and the Left an opportunity to perform and evaluated their work. For the BJP it is a clean slate, making the 2021 assembly polls a completely new game. It might be speculated that the Citizenship Amendment Act and the National Register of Citizens announced by the BJP's central government allegedly to drive a wedge between communities helped them rake up a larger vote share, but I would still argue that these announcements have very limited implications for the party as there are several other factors that finally matter.

During the Delhi elections, while my team was out on their field survey, I joined them and asked several voters from a cross-section of society what they thought of the Shaheen Bagh protest. A large number of them knew that there was such a protest going on, but they had no idea what it was all about. A forty-year-old male respondent from the lower economic strata pointed out that he was well taken care of by his chief minister, Arvind Kejriwal, who gave him free bijli–paani and free transport for his wife and that is why he would vote for him again. A cab driver, a street hawker and sundry others I met on the streets of Delhi time and again told us they were not interested in Shaheen Bagh or what it stood for. They worked hard to put food on the table and they wanted the government to not only supplement their incomes with welfare schemes but also ensure an environment of peace where they could work without any hindrances.

Communalism, hate speeches and a polarized campaign sure create an atmosphere but make no big impact. A couple of days after the Balakot strikes on 26 February 2019, there was the India Today conclave where I said that it would not impact the elections any more or less than what was panning out for the BJP. The founder-publisher of *India Today*, Aroon Purie, had sent me a letter saying he would hold me up to my words. I thankfully passed that test. During my election tours I have met a large section of voters whose livelihood depends on their daily wages. Whenever any agitation or violence takes place, that voter is the first to get affected. He is unable to make a living that day. Imagine going to bed hungry and worse if you have a family to feed. If the politics of struggle and strikes really worked, the communists would not have disappeared from the face of West Bengal. Nothing affects the common people like poor law and order or communal conflict and they are no longer putting up with that. Communal violence affects women voters the worst, who are worried about their own safety as well as about the loss of income due to poor law and order. When some antisocial elements and overzealous leaders make communal attacks or hate speeches, people judge their party for not taking the strictest action. If you do not punish them, you are backing them.

Religious leaders and extremists in both Hindu and Muslim communities keep themselves relevant by stoking the fire, but for political parties it barely earns any dividends. The media sure plays up India–Pakistan conflicts and communal violence because of the eyeballs that these issues draw, prompting many to believe that these are issues of top priority for every ordinary citizen. Nothing could be farther from the truth. The anti-CAA protests across the country and particularly Shaheen Bagh in Delhi is a shining example. The media coverage of Shaheen Bagh was far more than the development issues at stake like bijli–paani but finally people voted on the latter. Over the six months leading up to the Delhi polls, the BJP at the Centre had brought in a slew of big-ticket legislation such as the abrogation of Article 370, CAA and NRC and Ram Mandir at Ayodhya finally became a reality. If the Hindu–Muslim issue were such a big priority, the BJP had no reason to lose the Delhi polls. But it did and ignominiously so with just eight seats in its kitty.

Most politicians truly believe in the ideology of their party but they do not attribute victories and losses to stirring the communal pot. They usually represent a specific caste or community and hence for them it is vote bank politics. The Congress has played the secular card; Mayawati rides on Dalit sympathy; Mulayam Singh Yadav and Lalu Prasad Yadav have never lost sight of the Muslim–Yadav factor. The Hindu–Muslim binary does not work for all parties and politicians. If Hindutva and sharply communalized polls helped the BJP win the national and assembly polls since 2014, then how come the same party with the same ideology remained out of power for forty years since its inception?

The BJP's victory in the 2017 Uttar Pradesh assembly polls was attributed to the communal violence in Muzaffarnagar but there too I would insist it was the Modi government's good governance and the demonetization gambit of November 2016 that brought the party to power. In the last twenty years and at least five assembly elections in the state, Ram Mandir has always been the BJP's poll plank but it always drew a blank despite the polarization. So what did the BJP do differently this time? The note ban had a far-reaching impact on the poor of the country, who began looking at Modi as the one championing the cause of the less privileged and striking at the rich and their ill-gotten wealth. The BJP has also experienced the fallout of reverse consolidation – when the Hindus unite, so do the Muslims, a vote bank that Modi has been trying to win gradually with the abolition of triple talaq and other outreach programmes. He has also prioritized development over the mandir–masjid narrative and the returns were there to see for all. Nationalism makes for good living room conversation when one is well fed and rather meaningless for the hungry.

5

PM Contenders

National politics since 2014 has seen a leadership vacuum in the opposition as Prime Minister Narendra Modi, riding on his personal image, pulled off two back-to-back elections with a thumping majority. While he established himself as the sole leader within his party and won a sea of followers across the country and among the diaspora, some attribute his dominance to the TINA (there is no alternative) factor. So is there really no 'alternative'? Voices on the ground point to this.

Through my years of election-related travel, my interactions with voters have gone beyond the routine 'Iss baar kaun jeetega? [Who will win this time?]' I love getting an insight into human psychology and my interactions with voters present a great opportunity for me to learn more about the average Indian – how she feels, what moves her, what doesn't tick despite the government's best efforts, why the opposition fails when it does. Several times tall local leaders misread their popularity or the lack of it, but as a neutral outsider I, and of course my team, have caught the pulse of the people far more accurately. While leaders are usually misled by their coterie and yes-men, we have no blinkers and get a more panoramic view of the ground reality.

Before we address the 'who if not Modi' question, we must understand the political landscape of the country and the cultural context to our politics. If we were to divide the country into four regions, north and west put together have more than 60 per cent share of the total parliamentary seats, with east and south making up the rest, as this is based on the population distribution and density of the regions. This evidently tips the scale in favour of a leader who represents the north and west.

A second and very significant factor is language. The northern and western regions are dominantly Hindi-speaking or where Hindi is an acceptable language of communication. Even in states like Maharashtra, Rajasthan, Gujarat, Punjab and

Haryana, where regional languages dominate, Hindi-speaking leaders manage to connect with the masses. They see a Hindi-speaking leader, even if not from their own state, as one of them and as one worthy of representing their culture or concerns.

The geographical and cultural distance from south India has remained difficult to bridge. Also, the south's antipathy towards Hindi as a language has widened this north–south chasm. To my mind, while the southern states have thrown up several larger-than-life influential leaders who have held sway over their voters for decades, the north and west hold the key to Delhi's hot seat. Be it the corporate world, a family system or even federal government, the power centre remains where the core people belong. A prime ministerial candidate from the north and west fits in with the aspirations of the larger population, culturally and in terms of language, far more comfortably than one from the south. The location, population ratio and linguistic connect naturally favour leaders from these regions.

Though P.V. Narasimha Rao is a rare example of a leader from the south who held power as prime minister for a full term, he was not projected as the prime ministerial candidate to begin with. He became prime minister in the vacuum following Rajiv Gandhi's assassination. It is important to note how Rao managed to fit into the mould. He spoke seventeen languages fluently and, though he belonged to Andhra Pradesh, he had spread his wings and had won from the Ramtek parliamentary constituency in Maharashtra twice (1984 and 1989). He edged past other contenders in the party including Pranab Mukherjee and Sitaram Kesri with his deep understanding of the West and the Hindi heartland.

When we look at the current political milieu, it might seem there are barely any challengers to Prime Minister Modi. There are tall regional leaders like Mamata Banerjee, Sharad Pawar, Arvind Kejriwal, Nitish Kumar, Naveen Patnaik, who are unshakeable on their own turfs, but the question is, do they have that pan-Indian appeal? Former Congress chief Rahul Gandhi emerged as the sole contender to the prime ministerial post in 2019 and the rest is history. The Congress party's dearth of leadership is visible in their choices of Adhir Ranjan Chowdhury and previously Mallikarjun Kharge as the leader of the party in the Lok Sabha. Though there are popular youth leaders like Sachin Pilot, Gaurav Gogoi and until recently Jyotiraditya Scindia, they clearly lack the stature to take on a giant like Modi.

The Congress has failed to offer a strong contender to Modi especially since his rise in 2014 as Rahul Gandhi was never officially declared the prime ministerial candidate by the United Progressive Alliance. In the absence of any proven track record in an official position, Gandhi has not been taken seriously by the electorate. It is the media that has constantly pitted him against Modi and projected him as a prime ministerial candidate.

After years of good governance and a squeaky clean record, Bihar's 'sushasan babu' Nitish Kumar could have been a strong contender for a larger national role. What worked for him was the absence of 'family baggage'. The days of dynastic politics are behind us, precisely why Modi's biggest charm is his 'singlehood'. Politicians with their progeny in the same profession are often accused of nepotism and corruption. For example, for someone like H.D. Deve Gowda it was a recurrent nightmare that his family's shenanigans would sink his career. He even forewarned his principal secretary that if his family – or he himself under their pressure – sought any undue favours, they should be ignored.

Though Nitish Kumar has a son, he ensured there is little interference from him in his political work. Be it Lalu Prasad Yadav, who was formerly a friend, or Prashant Kishor or Modi, the moment Nitish feels his name is being sullied, he severs ties without a second thought. His aides Pavan Varma and George Fernandes too were cut off when they became difficult to deal with.

Except the fact that he lacked the backing of a robust organizational structure of a national party like the BJP or Congress, Nitish ticks nearly all the boxes – public image, delivery of promises, good governance, clean image, no family baggage and a dedicated following. If a comparative analysis were to be done for chief ministers of big states, Nitish, until his recent poll debacle, would have emerged as the front-runner in terms of his pan-Indian appeal. He fulfilled almost all the criteria that Modi did when he served as the chief minister of Gujarat. Of course Modi also had the blessing of a much larger national party and its ideological parent. But if we were to compare strictly on the basis of their personalities and merits, Nitish could have been a strong challenger to Modi. In 2014, when he vacated the chief minister's position for Jitan Ram Manjhi as he took responsibility for his party's poor showing in the parliamentary polls, only to be backstabbed by Manjhi, who wooed the BJP into an alliance sidelining Nitish, public sympathy soared for him. However, his popularity dipped drastically during the second half of his last tenure, roughly from the time he ditched his former allies, the Rashtriya Janata Dal and Congress, to join hands with the BJP, a move that was viewed as betrayal by voters of the Grand Alliance. The once-strong, decisive sushasan babu shockingly turned into a flip-flop chief minister, unwelcoming of the jobless, hapless daily wage workers trickling back to their home state due to a nationwide lockdown. Nitish lost huge political capital in the run-up to the assembly polls in 2020, one that the BJP could have swept if it had contested solo. Probably Nitish had gauged the chasm with the electorate well in advance and hence decided to hang up his boots after the assembly polls.

In a country that loves a 'bechara' candidate, there could be few more bechara than Nitish. He belongs to the 'other backward classes', keeps a low profile and is never seen flexing his political muscle for the wrong reasons. Modi too, in 2014, positioned himself as a bechara, recalling his days as the 'chaiwala' at a railway station. Modi not only made a pitch for pro-poor schemes during his 2014 poll campaign but also spent his first term in office as prime minister prioritizing several social welfare schemes like Ujjwala, Jan Dhan, Ayushman Bharat, Kisan Samman Nidhi and Swachh Bharat Abhiyan, schemes that helped him posture as the messiah of the marginalized. His first speech from the ramparts of the Red Fort on 15 August 2014 directly addressed the plight of women who had no toilets at home or had to use firewood for cooking instead of gas. The demonetization gambit too lured the have-nots as he seemed to take on the haves.

These instantly caught the imagination of the country that loved him and cheered him on for coming this far. And why not. Seventy per cent of India's population is underprivileged financially and socially. They are out of the mainstream and are themselves considered bechara. On the other hand, people who have led them for decades, their local representatives, are seen as powerful people, who on being elected became even more arrogant and inaccessible and amassed ill-gotten wealth. This underprivileged voter no longer associates with the rich and powerful politician and instead looks for one among them, 'apna aadmi', to represent their voices. They root for someone who understands their issues, culture, lifestyle and needs, and if they find that person they can relate to, there is no stopping them. Also, when their livelihood depends on the leader, they refuse to trust an entitled, privileged candidate, who is more likely to forget about the people and their expectations. Arvind Kejriwal's unassailable claim to the Delhi chief minister's seat is based purely on this. A middle-class, upper-caste, IIT graduate Indian Revenue Service officer fashioned himself into the affable aam aadmi with his muffler and flip-flops and addressed the masses in a conversational, easy-going manner. The autorickshaw drivers and the slum dwellers threw their weight behind Kejriwal just like years ago when cycle rickshaw pullers had helped Sharad Yadav first win from Jabalpur.

Now if a 'bechara' candidate gets the backing of a big party, his/her credibility and chances of victory become even stronger. Prime Minister Modi must have realized this much before any of us did and since his arrival in national politics he firmly sidelined leaders who were merely known for their right-wing ideology, particularly the old guard. Instead he stuck to his development agenda, all the while playing up on his image as one among the masses. People trusted him for his modest origins as he offered hope: 'If a chaiwala can become the prime minister of a country, then anyone can,' he often told them at rallies.

Through the centuries, not just in India but across the world, men have dominated leadership positions. Women are acutely aware of their disadvantage, even as they progress by leaps and bounds. The larger female electorate therefore connects well with the bechara candidates even more than men, who are socially better off in a patriarchal world. Modi, Naveen Patnaik, Kejriwal, Nitish, Mamata Banerjee, all have women voters strongly watching their backs. This is not true for someone like Vasundhara Raje Scindia, who despite being a woman is seen as a royal first. Jyotiraditya Scindia, who is known as Maharaj among his people, lost to the son of his father's accountant. In some sense, it was a verdict on his privilege.

Internal challengers to Modi within the BJP, say, leaders like Raman Singh, Shivraj Singh Chouhan and Vasundhara Raje, despite their long tenures as chief ministers and their acceptability in the Hindi heartland, did not show the same promise. Possibly their personalities faded in comparison to

Modi's, whose administrative strength at the Centre and equation with world leaders will remain the highlights of his tenure.

Regional satraps like Naveen Patnaik and Mamata Banerjee lose out heavily due to their inability to communicate well in Hindi. They are powerful leaders who connect with their own people, and while they could bring the opposition together and emerge as a consensus leader, they might never enjoy the same overwhelming support that Modi does when he reaches out to people across the country. Oratory sure is not the sole winning factor but a huge plus for mass leaders.

6

Indian Poor Vote More Than the Rich

How much we invest ourselves in something is directly proportional to how much that thing gives back to us. Politics is a patient witness of this give and take between political leaders and voters. Those who need or expect more from the leaders are more invested in realpolitik than those who have fewer expectations of or dependence on the government. Stands to reason why rural India votes in such large numbers and why posh South Mumbai's voter turnout rates are a national shame.

The underprivileged sections of society make sure they vote for the party or candidate who will address their issues and take care of their needs. They exercise their voting rights because they are dependent on the government for their livelihood and their elected representatives are their first port of call when in distress. They reach out to the local leaders with a genuine expectation that their grievances will be addressed. The rich, however, are not dependent on the outcome of the government in a similar manner. They are more occupied with other pursuits, related to work or leisure, and for them voting is not top priority. They vote only if it is convenient, in passing.

In India the definition of poor and rich is as shocking as the disparity of wealth distribution. Only around 6 per cent of the workforce in India file income tax returns.

While the underprivileged across the country choose to vote diligently, the geography of the region too has a bearing on the voting pattern. A look at voting trends shows how the voter turnout percentage gradually falls as one moves from the rural areas to a small town to a major town and a metro. In the 2019 assembly polls in Maharashtra, Aheri, a rural constituency, recorded a voter turnout of 70.35 per cent whereas in posh Colaba only 40 per cent of voters turned up to cast their ballot. In the 2018 Karnataka assembly polls, Tumkur Rural registered a voter turnout of 85.41 per cent while Bangalore South saw a low 52.86 per cent.

One reason for this is also that big cities have a large population of migrant workers who find it difficult to put their papers and documents together for want of a valid address or identity proof. Political parties too find it easier to mobilize masses in rural areas, where people are more closely knit. When grassroots workers reach out to voters in one village or one mohalla, they are able to mobilize the entire population in that area at one go. This, however, is not possible in a city where residents live in gated colonies and apartments and live aloof, isolated lives.

In a village or small town, sometimes even when there are multiple elections at one go, say, when the local assembly polls coincide with the gram, nagar or zila panchayat polls in which no election symbols are allotted, voters are fully aware of the candidates in the running in each of these elections and can easily identify them by their names. That is the level of awareness and interest of voters in the electoral process in the rural parts of the country – and why not, their daily lives are tied to the outcome of these polls.

If we look at India as a whole, voter turnout is higher in the states where urbanization is less. Let's compare Madhya Pradesh and Maharashtra and we will see a stark difference. MP has a largely rural population and in the absence of adequate private jobs there is more dependence on the rural economy. In the MP assembly polls in December 2018, the voter turnout was a whopping 74.61 per cent against Maharashtra's 2019 assembly polls where the voter turnout was only 61.13 per cent.

In the general elections of 2019, the all-India voter turnout stood at 67.11 per cent. As mentioned earlier, in India 70 per cent voters are rural and the rest are urban. Of the 70 per cent, approximately 75 per cent go out to vote, which accounts for 52 per cent across India. In the urban areas the average turnout is usually roughly 50 per cent, which makes it 15 per cent across India, adding up to 67 per cent approximately.

Tall leaders like Indira Gandhi and Narendra Modi read these trends and modelled their governance accordingly. Any leader who has addressed this section of the electorate has enjoyed very long tenures, for example, Jawaharlal Nehru, Jyoti Basu and Indira Gandhi. In the 1990s *India Today* conducted a survey on the best prime minister of India till then and Nehru won hands down. He remained popular for generations after, and his winning streak can be credited to his pro-poor outlook.

Leaders like Jyoti Basu, Naveen Patnaik, Manik Sarkar, M.G. Ramachandran, Raman Singh, Shivraj Singh Chouhan, Jayalalithaa and Narendra Modi kept being voted back to power as chief ministers because they addressed the concerns of the poor and never neglected this key vote bank. The National Rural Employment Guarantee Act was a clear-cut winner for Prime Minister Manmohan Singh when he introduced it in 2005.

While only the relatively rich pay income tax, the poor also contribute to the exchequer through the goods and services tax (GST) and other indirect taxes. For any government it is imperative to look after its people; however, not everyone is dependent on the government in a similar manner. The delivery of power, water and roads (bijli, paani, sadak) affects everyone. The rich use these amenities as much as the poor do. But public education, healthcare facilities and law and order touch only certain segments. The rich can afford expensive private schools and colleges or send their kids abroad. They can get the best medical treatment despite the costs involved and are free to hire their own security guards. The poor depend heavily on the government for good education, medical attention and for a peaceful life.

We have often seen and read how the privileged get away even when they are on the wrong side of the law and the poor suffer for no fault of theirs. A strong government that fixes loopholes in the policing system and ensures a safe environment for its people has always been more popular with the poorer sections. However, for them the first basic expectation is that the government of the day should provide livelihood support. The rich may prioritize anything from pollution levels to the traffic situation, gardens and garbage collection, cleanliness, tax regime or overall infrastructure.

While the decisions of any government affect people uniformly, at times it is like a see-saw. A move that works remarkably well for the poor does the very opposite for the privileged and vice versa. This analogy might not always work but when it is at play the government's job to strike a balance becomes even tougher. Modi's demonetization gambit is a big case in point.

Before talking about the impact of demonetization, let us rewind a bit and look at Modi and his takeover of the party at the national level. Modi was acutely aware of the BJP's 'pro-rich, pro-urban and pro-upper caste' image. Even today political analysts will tell you how the party does remarkably better in urban pockets and big cities compared to the rural belts. When Modi took charge, he knew he had to shed that public perception if he was to govern sustainably and for long. He knew the tried-and-tested strategy of the past is the key to governing India but the shift from pro-rich to pro-poor and pro-urban to pro-rural could not come overnight. Modi began giving the BJP an image makeover by hard-selling his own 'chaiwala' days and reiterating his humble origins. While the setting of his birth was not the rustic village, he recreated the imagery of a young boy scurrying along a railway platform handing out cups of hot tea to passengers. When he juxtaposed his days of hardship with the privileges of a dynast, he instantly connected with the masses, which forgot the privileged past of the BJP and its founders. Modi held out the promise of looking after the poor mothers in the villages, not letting them suffer in the kitchen smoke, symbolic of their domestic drudgery. He promised dignity to women by building them toilets. He sought sixty months as opposed to the sixty years of Congress rule and held up Gujarat as the model of governance.

After a thumping majority in the parliamentary polls of 2014, Modi seemed to be on a winning spree, winning Maharashtra, Jharkhand and Haryana that year. Though I would attribute those victories to a revolving door theory as the states were just itching for a change. In 2015, when President Barack Obama visited India, Modi was sucked into a controversy with his fancy hologram suit and Maybach glasses. The opposition made hay while the sun shone on them through the following months. Modi's popularity took a hit for the first time and consequent losses in Delhi and Bihar polls made it worse. Despite Lalu Prasad Yadav's corrupt image, his alliance with Nitish Kumar sailed through. Kejriwal wooed the common man while Modi yet again fell into the perception trap and the states went to opposition parties one after the other. Even as Modi rolled out his pro-poor schemes like the Jan Dhan Yojana, the Ujjwala scheme and housing for all, the string of losses continued.

It was in that backdrop that on 8 November 2016 Modi appeared before a national audience to announce what would be a huge game changer for him for years to come. Modi's promise to bring back black money and deposit Rs 15 lakh in every citizen's account had begun to be touted as a 'jumla'. The promise was to check the circulation of black money and the said Rs 15 lakh was just a metaphor. The mathematics was never that simple. But in the face of mounting pressure, Modi decided to target the rich, the traders and black money holders, and overnight became the messiah of the poor. At the time the note ban weakened the position of the business houses, traders and politicians whereas for the poor it might at best have been some sort of harassment to get their old notes exchanged for new currency notes. The poor live on daily wages and had few savings to lose. But even in those serpentine queues outside banks, the poor and the middle class rarely spoke against the note ban.

Interestingly, the timing of the demonetization was close to the Uttar Pradesh assembly elections slated for March 2017 in which incumbent chief minister Akhilesh Yadav had begun to come across as a strong contender owing to his satisfactory governance. The note ban was probably an image correction effort as much as it was to convey to the people that Modi had always been serious about bringing back black money. The move worried those who had stacks of cash, but the underprivileged stood on the fringes gleefully watching the plight of the haves. What worked like a dream in this gambit was how money started flowing into the accounts of the poor as the black money hoarders tried to save their cash by diverting it into the accounts of their domestic help and other staff. Even as the poor were told that this money would have to be eventually returned and that it did not belong to them, the joy of seeing one's account swell is indescribable. The poor are a victim of the arrogance of the rich but with the latter now turning to them for desperate help tipped the uneven scales in favour of the poor. While it was beyond their expectations that their accounts would have lakhs of rupees, the thrill of seeing the employer or the local heavyweight beseeching them was overwhelming. And once the money goes into someone else's account you cannot even mistreat them. I have heard several first-hand experiences to say this with much certainty that a large number of people who rescued their richer acquaintances, employers, friends, felt 'if not Rs 15 lakh, at least something has come into my account' and that Modi finally did it.

We did a survey before the UP elections on whether demonetization was a good idea and there was a clear indication that people voted in its favour.

Around 57 per cent of the respondents said it was a good decision, 30 per cent said it was a bad decision, 11 per cent said it had no impact and 2 per cent remained undecided. Demonetization worked like a dream for Modi and I would say even the 2019 parliamentary poll victory can be partially attributed to it.

7

Dynasty Is Dead and Criminality Is Heading the Same Way

From a time when politics was a dirty word to an anti-corruption movement that saw scores of young professionals give up their lucrative careers to enter active politics, the profession has come a long way. Politicians are acutely aware of their privileges, particularly if they come from an established political family, and know that their position is more precarious than that of a rookie politician, who gets to start off on a clean slate. The dynasty system in politics has run its course and 'raja ka beta hi raja hoga' no longer holds true.

The communication era of the 1980s and 1990s gave voters a peek into the lives of dynasts and non-dynasts. The stark differences are apparent and well defined. Be it the Abdullahs and Muftis in Jammu and Kashmir, Scindias in Madhya Pradesh, Chavans and Thackerays in Maharashtra, Mulayam Singh Yadav and Lalu Prasad Yadav in the Hindi heartland, Deve Gowda and Karunanidhi in the south, wherever one turned there were deeply embedded political families that almost monopolized the profession. Only in states with dominant Left parties were there no dynastic politics and the then fledgling BJP was run by first-generation politicians.

Starting in the late 1990s, with the BJP ruling for some six years under Atal Bihari Vajpayee, a bachelor with no strings attached, people started believing that if a person does not have family baggage, he is likely to serve the people more honestly. The seeds of anti-dynast sentiments that were sown back then gradually led to a general preference for non-dynast, honest, promising young newcomers, whose lives seemed more relatable. They emerged as one of the people, their struggles, their understanding of the stark realities, their conviction to bring change seemed real, genuine.

The final rejection of the dynasts came almost two decades later, in 2019 when some of the tallest dynasts fell. Rahul Gandhi, Jyotiraditya Scindia, Bhupinder Singh Hooda, R.P.N. Singh, H.D.

Kumaraswamy's son Nikhil Gowda, Ashok Chavan and several members of Sharad Pawar's family, all faced ignominious losses. These families had never previously lost elections, not in their own strong bastions, some of which they had held for almost five decades. What does it indicate? People were evidently looking for change, for someone from among themselves. The dominant belief was 'If a chaiwala can win, then any of us can'. That sparked the rise of the poor, underprivileged, bechara candidate against a dynast. Voters strongly felt a connection with the non-dynast, valued his/her understanding of the lives of the poor and was convinced they had better insight into the issues of the poor. The dynast reared in a protected environment laden with privileges became the 'other', the outsider who seemed to have no understanding of the issues of the poor.

Third-generation voters, unlike their parents and grandparents, also did not share the same connect or affiliation with the political families that ruled in the 1960s, 1970s or 1980s. Having left their home towns to pursue careers that took them to other cities, they were no longer directly dependent on these political families for their livelihood. The ones who stayed back and looked up to these families also could no longer relate to the dynasts, who were nothing like their fathers or the previous generation. Their lifestyle was different, they no longer spoke the local dialect fluently, their English was accented, their mannerisms alien. During one of our pre-poll surveys – and I would not want to name the politician – the locals, who were otherwise staunch supporters of the political family, told us, 'Arrey woh toh sirf hawai jahaaz se aate jaate hain,' clearly unhappy with his 'high-flying' ways. The disconnect has been on both ends. When the most prominent dynast of our times lost the family bastion of Amethi to a political novice, it was a resounding death knell for all dynasts. If a Gandhi can lose, anyone can lose.

The way a non-dynast can mingle with the crowd or pander to their feelings, a dynast just can't. The way Prime Minister Narendra Modi washed the feet of a Dalit in one of his rallies during the 2019 polls, a dynast would not even think of doing such a thing or would struggle to pull it off. Not because he is arrogant but because it does not fit into his family's image or his narrative. There are legit limitations. There is the baggage of the past. These are burdens that a dynast can never shed, at least not in the blink of an eye. When will people stop asking Rahul Gandhi uncomfortable questions about the Emergency? For other dynasts it is the baggage of non-performance of their family members. The new candidate has a clean slate, and fairly so.

Voters have also begun to assume that a political family will indulge in corruption and nepotism to keep themselves relevant, powerful and afloat. Even tall, established leaders are being rejected, especially if they have a son following in their footsteps. At times the sons have failed to add to their political capital or goodwill. Even a Vilasrao Deshmukh, whose son had nothing to do with politics, was brought down by his son's foolhardy adventure into the post-26/11 ruins at the terror-hit Taj and Oberoi hotels. Daughters have been a boon in that sense. Look at the Nationalist Congress Party chief Sharad Pawar, whose daughter Supriya Sule has kept his ship sailing, and how. Even better off are those who have no progeny at all. No one hurls corruption or moneylaundering charges at Modi or Naveen Patnaik. 'After all, who will they amass all the wealth for?' they ask.

However, the question before the youth today is, can politics be a sustainable career choice? The image of the quintessential politician is one of a powerful, corrupt, filthy-rich political heavyweight.

While this may attract a newcomer, the real test is winnability, for which a candidate needs to be a credible, trustworthy face. This same credibility is lost in the lust for money or on the path to become that quintessential politician, who is now falling out of favour. Modi's back-to-back victories have restored many voters' faith in honest politics and that it could be a good career opportunity if one is honest and is committed to serve the people. The emergence of a new generation of politicians from the hallowed portals of the Indian Institute of Technology, such as Arvind Kejriwal, Manohar Parrikar, Jairam Ramesh, who pretty much have a clean track record and high credibility, has inspired many young men and women who would otherwise have never given politics a serious thought. Today they can cite these examples when their parents root for a stable career.

Unemployment is another reason the youth join politics. They begin as grassroots workers and work their way up in the party organization. Unlike in the olden days, party workers down to the last rung now draw salaries, even if small, and are reimbursed for their out-of-pocket expenses. This has led to larger cadres who are committed to building party membership and they view their political work as a steady job whereas earlier it was considered political activism. Politicians too have realized the significance of a strong presence on the ground and hire large teams to make sure their connect with the people is never lost.

At the time of the freedom struggle, political work and going to jail on charges of civil disobedience and sedition were a matter of pride. It drew sympathy and admiration in equal measure from fellow patriots. Over time, politics became a dirty word associated with muscle and money power, and going to jail again became the norm, just that this time it was on corruption charges, violence or for criminal activities. In twenty-first-century India, following the anti-corruption movement, consensus is building over cleansing politics from within. The rejection of dynasts, the rise of politicians like Modi from a humble background and the influx of professionals in political parties have ushered in a new dawn for Indian politics. So much so that the Supreme Court in a directive in February 2020 ordered political parties to publish the criminal history of their candidates before a parliamentary or assembly election. This transparency has long been sought by the people, and several non-governmental organizations have already been drawing up their own fact sheets to put these details out before the voter.

The rejection of criminals in politics is slower than that of dynasts, but it is on the rise. However, there is no denying that several political heavyweights facing the worst criminal charges are also some of the most discerning and well-connected politicians. There are tall leaders who have criminal or corruption charges against them, but these leaders are also extremely well connected with their loyal voter base. They take good care of their voters by bringing in welfare schemes for them. Some leaders also manage to win elections because of the fear factor, flexing their muscles in their constituencies. But my personal belief remains that this species is on the verge of extinction.

With a marked shift in the expectations of the people, the electoral environment has also changed. The election process has become far more transparent and robust. Gone are the days of booth capturing and meddling with ballot boxes. The polling and counting process through electronic voting machines (EVMs) is foolproof, regardless of the allegations by several opposition parties. I can say so with some degree of authority because the election results and our pre-poll surveys mostly tie in perfectly. Our surveys are conducted face to face and more than 95 per cent of our predictions match with what the EVMs eventually reveal. I would really be way off the mark if the EVMs were tampered with. Only losers talk of faulty EVMs but there is no tangible proof that the results can be changed with any jugglery. In fact, several delegations from foreign countries come to India to learn the process of working these EVMs and how our elections are carried out.

The Election Commission must be lauded for rolling out a mammoth exercise in the world's largest democracy with such accuracy. Of course electoral reforms should always be welcomed and there is no room for complacency. There are loopholes that can always be plugged. For instance, the voter turnout should be announced within 2–3 hours after voting concludes but this usually comes after 24 hours. This leaves a nagging doubt in the minds of the political parties and analysts over possible foul play and also makes our lives as pollsters difficult, but that is another story!

8

Crowds at Rallies Don't Mean Victory

Ahead of the 2014 parliamentary polls when debutant prime ministerial candidate Narendra Modi held whirlwind tours and addressed massive gatherings across states, his audiences scaled buildings, walls and hoardings to get a glimpse of the rising national star. They listened to him with rapt attention, cheering out of turn, breaking into rapturous applause at his sharp jibes against the incumbent United Progressive Alliance government. The crowds just went wild with Modi's appearance on the podium. Did that reflect his influence over the people? Most certainly. Did that mean the BJP would win? Well, maybe. Did that mean all the candidates he was campaigning for in each of those rallies would win comfortably? Not really.

Rallies are all about fun, festivity and funds and have little or almost no impact on the voting choices of people. A massive, bustling public meeting is not indicative of a candidate's bright prospects. It merely means that the local organization of the party is robust or that the party/candidate has adequate funds to mobilize the local electorate to show up for a few hours in their support. The rally's strength or success has no bearing whatsoever on how those same voters will vote. Because the choices are not dependent on what they hear at the rally but on what has been driven home through the campaign and of course on other factors like a promising leader at the helm of the party, connect with the local leadership, caste or community equations and the like.

Back in the early years after Independence, people were keen to listen to their leaders but hardly had the opportunity. Speeches by the prime minister or president trickled in on the radio on special occasions like Independence Day and Republic Day or in case of an emergency. There was no way of seeing or listening to them up close like we do in the age of social media. But because the communication was so restricted and the platforms so limited, leaders as well as voters took public rallies far more seriously. Leaders were careful about what they projected before the audience. They weighed their words, knowing they would be held accountable for their statements. It was also their primary image-building exercise and hence they were cautious not to make irresponsible statements, unlike leaders today who have the luxury of explaining their bloopers during speeches at rallies and public meetings by tweeting or posting on Facebook or issuing a press statement. Rallies have also lost their appeal as the communication gap between the voter and the candidate stands bridged today. Voters get to interact directly with their leaders on Twitter and Facebook and through live interactive videos across platforms. Technology has enabled the voter to reach out directly to the topmost leaders in the country, who have learned to use social media platforms to their advantage. While young and old alike use smartphones today and are connected with the larger community through popular platforms like WhatsApp, Facebook and YouTube, in several households where the elderly are not familiar with technology, they depend on second-hand information from the youth in the family. The youth influence decision-making by relaying trends and moods they pick up through social media.

Every time the prime minister follows someone on Twitter, he also manages to reach out to that entire community, region or profession. It appears as though he has a direct connect with the masses and this portrays him as a people's person. Social media has effectively rendered public rallies redundant because the leaders have several other channels of communication that are more personal and intimate. The impersonal nature of public rallies does not help in creating any connect with the masses.

Moreover, not all rallies can be held on a Sunday or a holiday and elections are scheduled such that they do not happen around festivals. On working days it is next to impossible to get people in the metros to skip work and turn up for a rally during the day. They are held in the evenings, by when people are tired after a hard day's work, especially with all the big city commute. Even in smaller towns, it is very difficult to mobilize voters on a working day. In the summers, crowds get restless during the long wait ahead of a leader's arrival at the rally and the organizers are only too eager to tell you about the anxiety they go through while holding the people back. Yet politicians love their moment in front of a massive gathering. Rallies also help political parties amplify their campaigns, especially those around tall leaders like the prime minister, chief ministers or popular national leaders. It gives them good publicity, value for money I would say, as news channels are keen to livecast speeches from rallies of key leaders like Narendra Modi, Rahul Gandhi, Mamata Banerjee, Mayawati and Arvind Kejriwal. Even amid the nationwide lockdown due to Covid-19, rallies continued to be held through the Bihar assembly polls and ahead of the West Bengal polls, violating all physical distancing guidelines.

Earlier people endured all the discomfort in the hope they would get to hear their leader directly but now as politicians speak at multiple platforms there is no novelty left in a speech at a rally. Speeches at rallies, much like manifestos, are taken with a pinch of salt. Voters are jaded by now, thanks to all the years of false promises by our politicians. The release of a manifesto has become a mere formality and in some elections they are made public barely a few days before polling. In the 2014 parliamentary polls, the BJP released its manifesto in the north-eastern states after the first phase of polling. So, well, that is how much we value that document.

However, rallies are undeniably great fun, almost like the annual village fair, as long as it is not the parliamentary elections, which are held in peak summer. Free rides to the venue, food packets and a token amount, however, make the effort worth it, not to mention the picnic that it finally turns out to be! My guesstimate is not even 10 per cent of the crowd that claps and cheers for the leader in question will vote for him/her on the basis of what they hear at the rally. On several occasions, political leaders tell me, 'Oh, I held such a big rally but your poll says something else . . . you must have got it wrong. If so many connected with us, how can they not vote for us!' I have a standard reply to this. Let the results speak. I have, in most cases, had the last laugh. The recent Delhi assembly polls witnessed an aggressive campaign on a massive scale by the BJP that pulled out all stops. From the prime minister to union ministers, chief ministers of BJP-ruled states and the party's high-profile star campaigners, all were roped in. There were reports that 200 BJP parliamentarians stayed overnight at the various slums to connect with the voters. Prime Minister Modi, who had just about nine months before that swept all seven parliamentary seats in Delhi, held bustling rallies in the national capital. The poll results showed none of this had any impact on the people's choices. The AAP that was expected to suffer some degree of anti-incumbency instead enjoyed a pro-incumbency based solely on Arvind Kejriwal's delivery of basic amenities, some pro-people decisions on pilgrimage for the elderly, revamped public schools, mohalla clinics and free bijli–paani. This was a clear verdict that no amount of resources and muscle power can outweigh good governance and strong delivery. The BJP sure grabbed eyeballs in the run-up to the polls, captured a chunkier space in the local newspapers and created more noise but none of that paid off. Had the BJP managed to punch holes in Kejriwal's claims of good governance and also had a better counteroffer for the people, it may have had a fighting chance. But its campaign revolved around high-pitched yet hollow rhetoric that had absolutely no impact on the voters. The BJP should have learned its lesson from the campaign in Bihar in 2015 when too its so-called nationalistic campaign had boomeranged. 'Pakistan mein phatake phootenge' did them no good and an unlikely coalition of Nitish Kumar's JD(U) and Lalu Prasad Yadav's RJD swept the state. During the Bihar assembly elections of 2020, the mood on the ground was the veritable opposite of what the BJP had witnessed in 2015. RJD chief Tejashwi Yadav's rallies were thronging with people whereas Nitish Kumar and other tall NDA leaders got booed in their rallies. The election outcome was very different. The NDA emerged victorious, which could be attributed to Modi's delivery at the Centre and Nitish's liquor ban in the state. Women in particular voted heavily in favour of the NDA and they came out in large numbers to make their vote count. This turned out to be a huge game changer. The massive crowds at the rallies of Tejashwi and Mahagathbandhan leaders ultimately made no difference to their prospects.

In Delhi, the BJP has been sitting in the opposition for over twenty years now despite its strong hold on the municipal corporations. In the 2020 assembly polls, it had the advantage of being in power at the Centre while the opposition space seemed like a vacuum in the absence of Congress stalwart Sheila Dikshit.

For a party that had won 67 out of 70 seats in its second electoral contest, repeating a similar feat was a huge achievement. The 62 seats the AAP won in its third outing at the 'ballot box office' is a hard lesson for its political opponents.

Voters today are so clued in that they are able to evaluate the track records of the candidates and parties and make an informed choice. The allegations against the AAP that they spent a substantial amount of public money in publishing advertisements did not raise any hackles, well, because if you have worked hard then what's the harm publicizing it! Voters today ask a very basic question in response to most government decisions – is this good for me? If the answer is in the negative, they wait for the next opportunity to show their leaders the door. There is no room for second chances for a non-performing government any longer.

Seasoned politicians are acutely aware of this. In the 2013 assembly polls in Madhya Pradesh, Shivraj Singh Chouhan, even after his seven-year stint as chief minister, made it a ritual to rattle off his government's achievements for the first 40 minutes in every public rally. Only after that did he move on to new promises. He strictly abstained from mud-slinging and hurling allegations at his opponents. When reporters asked him why he did not attack his rivals, he would say, 'First let me finish talking about my work, I can talk about others later.' This surely worked, for the BJP won three consecutive elections under Chouhan, each with a bigger mandate than before. At that point, the BJP had no national visibility and Chouhan's success was his alone. That is also the thing about positive campaigns. They almost always leave a warm, fuzzy feeling among voters.

9

GDP and Stock Market Figures Have No Bearing on Poll Prospects

Ahead of every parliamentary poll there is a common chatter in the plush living rooms of big city dwellers – that the state of the economy will have a direct impact on the poll prospects of the incumbent government. But after every such election, the prediction is invariably proved wrong. If we examine the general elections of the last two decades, each one of them has defied this common perception and for fairly good reasons. The Bihar assembly polls that gave the JD(U)–BJP combine a narrow but clear victory – leaving us pollsters, who had predicted a decisive win for the Mahagathbandhan, at our wits' end – in an environment of economic gloom and a steady fall in the gross domestic product (GDP) bears testimony to the fact that the economy – at least as rich urbanites understand it – has no bearing on poll results. To my mind, the impact of the Covid-19 pandemic upon the state coffers over a reasonably long period of time could alter this trend but not any time soon.

To understand why this is so, we need to look at how the various sectors contribute to our economy and their reach in terms of the voting population that is involved in that sector. Despite being a 'krishi pradhan' (agriculture-dominated) country, India draws only 15.87 per cent of its GDP from agriculture, even as a sizeable section of its voting population (roughly 80 per cent) earns at least part of their livelihood from agriculture and allied services. In sharp contrast, the services sector, which is the largest contributor to our GDP at a whopping 54.4 per cent (2018–19), remains concentrated in twenty to thirty cities while industry contributes 29.73 per cent. The services sectors like information technology, courier, media and entertainment and banking are clustered in some metros and tier I and II cities like Delhi, Mumbai, Bengaluru, Hyderabad, Ahmedabad and Pune. It is only in unprecedented times like the Covid-19 pandemic that we witnessed migrant labour distressed and displaced during the initial nationwide lockdown.

Even if we were to assume that the 4.68 crore migrant labour in the country affected during the Covid-19 crisis were upset with the government's handling of their situation or the economy, that population is only a fraction of the total 25 crore households that end up voting. The impact is not more than 20 per cent but let us also not forget that only 50 to 60 per cent of the urban voters cast their ballot. If the migrant worker population is happy with the state of the economy then there could be some impact on the economy, nonetheless marginal in my opinion. Overall, whether the economy does well or poorly, either way it has hardly any impact on poll results.

A look at election outcomes over the last two decades summarizes my arguments succinctly. The backdrop of the 2004 'India Shining' poll campaign led by then prime minister Atal Bihari Vajpayee showcased his much-hyped economic optimism. The GDP growth rate that year was on a high at 7.92 per cent and there was a general consensus on the economy faring well under Vajpayee. Yet he lost to the United Progressive Alliance and fell sharply from his previous tally of 182 seats to 135. Andhra Pradesh emerged as a microcosm of the same phenomenon that was playing out at the national level. Despite Chandrababu Naidu's stellar performance in the state with a booming IT industry – the emergence of Satyam as a big player (this is back when Satyam was an IT icon rather than a scandal), setting up of Ramoji City, etc. – the chief minister, whose party was the second largest in the NDA coalition government of 1999, flopped, and how. Conversely, in 2009, when the world was going through one of its worst recessions, Prime Minister Manmohan Singh comfortably led the UPA to a second term. Again, in Andhra Pradesh at that time, Y.S. Rajasekhara Reddy, who was seen as a leader of farmers – unlike Naidu, who was a mascot of growth and technology – steered his party to a clear victory and also contributed heavily to the UPA, sending 33 MPs to the Centre from the 42 seats in the state.

In 2014, despite a GDP growth rate of 7.41 per cent, a 1.02 per cent increase compared to the previous year, the Manmohan Singh government crumbled to debutant Narendra Modi. The 2019 general elections stood testimony once again to the fact that the state of the economy does not change a party's prospects. The Modi government came back stronger at a time the economy plummeted to an eleven-year low of a 5.02 per cent GDP growth rate.

A wobbly economy does not necessarily mean huge cuts in public spending and, as I stated earlier, all governments, at the Centre or state, are judged entirely on their 'delivery', that is, essentially pro-poor policies and social security spending. One can argue that if the economy is not doing well then tax collections are also badly hit, but the question is 'how badly'. For if government tax collections are below expectations, the defence budget can always be trimmed as a first measure. If you look at the global scenario in such years, then warlike situations usually do not arise in such circumstances/recession years. Even in the Covid-19 crisis, India and China would not want to wage war, regardless of their political posturing. Central and state governments also look at quick revenue raisers such as collections from alcohol, which became a saviour during the early nationwide lockdown days across states. Petrol/diesel taxes have also been a source of increased revenue collection during the recent economic slowdown.

Effectively, public spending is hardly affected unless an unforeseen crisis like the Covid-19 pandemic wreaks havoc on the economy and the government is forced to rework its priorities. But, in a low-growth year, even if business houses are affected, their profit percentage may have gone down but they would still have made a profit that year. No loss or even a low profit rate leaves a sentiment of loss in the business community that in turn impacts their advertising and media spending and the latter takes it upon itself to amplify a sense of doom among the people. The common man mostly remains untouched by this but the perception creators in the media studios cry themselves hoarse because their revenue that comes from corporates and business houses is curtailed. Voters on the ground have nothing to do with this perception and hence their preferences see no change. For farmers, monsoons are a huge factor and a drought or hailstorm would hit their pockets. Elections could sway in an altogether different direction if the incumbent government does not pay attention to farmers' demands in such a situation or if the opposition makes a more credible promise. The longer-term political impact of the ongoing farmers' protests remains to be seen. We can never deny the existence of two Indias – a krishi pradhan Bharat and a more elite India – both of which have different sets of priorities and both of which vote differently.

Analysts and intellectuals often compare our voting pattern with that of the United States where there is a direct connection between the health of the economy and the prospect of the incumbent government. But what we do not take into account is that in the Indian context even if out of every Rs 100 only Rs 16 comes from the rural sector the dominant 80 per cent vote bank also comes from this sector. The American economy, on the other hand, is substantially driven by the insurance section, be it general, medical or life insurance. A fall in the stock market affects most Americans as their savings are invested directly or indirectly in stocks – unlike in India where only a small percentage owns stocks. Most working Americans depend on their jobs for medical insurance and losing a job can mean losing access to healthcare. If the economy goes down, then sentiments begin to change on the ground as everyone across the board stands affected and the incumbent government becomes the first victim of a raging negative sentiment. Considering the contributors to the GDP in the two countries are so different, it is a rather unfair and inaccurate comparison to make. India's per capita GDP (nominal) is around $2000 while that of the US is over $60,000. The needs and priorities of the majority are totally different in the two countries.

As I have argued at length earlier, election outcomes depend largely on parameters such as roads, electricity, water supply, inflation, unemployment, law and order situation and farmer-related issues. In this seventy-fourth year of independence, roads and electricity connections are by and large taken care of across the country while drinking water continues to be a huge crisis in some states. Inflation and unemployment have a direct connection with the state of the economy. When we say the economy is doing well, the general sense is that prices are going up, be it of real estate or anything at all and vice versa. If the economy fares badly, prices go down, businesses do poorly and a pall of gloom descends with rising job cuts and unemployment. But this unemployment affects about a 5 crore population working in the urban cities in the services and manufacturing sectors. It is such a minuscule fraction of the actual voting population that a negative sentiment against the incumbent government barely has any impact on the election outcome. Though the opposite may not always be true. A happy business community, migrant labour and service class could help the same incumbent nudge through close margins too.

India is not only the world's largest democracy but also by far the most diverse. No one statement can hold true for all voters or groups of voters. In this book I have tried to examine the sentiments of all sections of voters: whether urban, rural, poor, middle class, elite, men or women. What matters to them, how they see politics, how they choose their leaders and how likely they are to vote. The debates and topics covered by news media at times typically may reflect the interests or priorities of only a certain section of voters.

Discussions about communalism or GDP growth are far removed from the issues that will really decide who wins or loses an election. Our experience of conducting surveys across the length and breadth of India since 2013, and our focus on truly understanding the mind of the voter, has shown us that what ultimately matters most is delivery.

Appendix

Axis MY INDIA – Track Record

No. of Elections Including 2014 & 2019 GE	Most Accurate Predictions
52	48

92% + Accuracy rate

Appendix

2013 – Assembly Election

8 December 2013

MADHYA PRADESH (AE 2013) – 230 Seats			
PARTY	BJP	INC	OTHERS
Axis MY INDIA Predictions	162	60	8
RESULTS	165	58	7

8 December 2013

CHHATTISGARH (AE 2013) – 90 Seats			
PARTY	BJP	INC	OTHERS
Axis MY INDIA Predictions	48	38	4
RESULTS	49	39	2

8 December 2013

DELHI (AE 2013) – 70 Seats				
PARTY	BJP	INC	AAP	OTHERS
Axis MY INDIA Predictions	24	17	27	2
RESULTS	32	8	28	2

8 December 2013

RAJASTHAN (AE 2013) – 200 Seats			
PARTY	BJP	INC	OTHERS
Axis MY INDIA Predictions	106	78	16
RESULTS	163	21	16

Appendix

2014 – Assembly Election

19 October 2014

MAHARASHTRA (AE 2014) – 288 Seats					
PARTY	BJP	SHIV SENA	INC	NCP	OTHERS
Axis MY INDIA Predictions	98–108	84–93	43–48	33–38	15
RESULTS	122	63	42	41	20

19 October 2014

HARYANA (AE 2014) – 90 Seats					
PARTY	INLD	BJP	INC	HJC (BL)	OTHERS
Axis MY INDIA Predictions	31–35	29–33	18–20	3	4
RESULTS	19	47	15	2	7

23 December 2014

JHARKHAND (AE 2014) – 81 Seats						
PARTY	BJP	AJSU	INC	JVM	JMM	OTHERS
Axis MY INDIA Predictions	34–38	3–5	4–6	12–16	10–14	7–14
RESULTS	37	5	5	8	19	7

23 December 2014

J&K (AE 2014) – 87 Seats					
PARTY	PDP	BJP	INC	JKNC	OTHERS
Axis MY INDIA Predictions	36–41	16–22	9–13	9–13	6–10
RESULTS	28	25	12	15	7

Appendix

2014 – General Election

16 May 2014

LOK SABHA ELECTION 2014 – 543 Seats				
PARTY	NDA	UPA	LEFT	OTHERS
Axis MY INDIA Predictions	287	107	25	124
RESULTS	336	59	11	137

Appendix

2015 – Assembly Election

10 February 2015

DELHI (AE 2015) – 70 Seats				
PARTY	BJP	INC	AAP	OTHERS
Axis MY INDIA Predictions	17±7	0–2	53±7	0
RESULTS	3	0	67	0

8 November 2015

BIHAR (AE 2015) – 243 Seats			
PARTY	JD(U)+	BJP+	OTHERS
Axis MY INDIA Predictions	169–183	58–70	3–7
RESULTS	178	58	7

Appendix

2016 – Assembly Election

19 May 2016

ASSAM (AE 2016) – 126 Seats							
PARTY	BJP+	BJP	AGP	BPF	INC	AIUDF	OTHERS
Axis MY INDIA Predictions	79–93	56–65	13–16	10–12	26–33	6–10	1–4
RESULTS	86	60	14	12	26	13	1

19 May 2016

KERALA (AE 2016) – 140 Seats				
PARTY	LDF	UDF	BJP	OTHERS
Axis MY INDIA Predictions	88–101	38–48	0–3	1–4
RESULTS	91	47	1	1

19 May 2016

PUDUCHERRY (AE 2016) – 30 Seats				
PARTY	INC + DMK	AINRC	AIADMK	OTHERS
Axis MY INDIA Predictions	15–21	8–12	1–4	0–2
RESULTS	17	8	4	1

Appendix

19 May 2016

WEST BENGAL (AE 2016) – 294 Seats					
PARTY	TMC	LEFT + INC	BJP	GOJAM	OTHERS
Axis MY INDIA Predictions	233–253	38–51	1–5	3	2
RESULTS	**211**	**76**	**3**	**3**	**1**

19 May 2016

TAMIL NADU (AE 2016) – 232 / 234 Seats				
PARTY	AIADMK	DMK + INC	BJP	OTHERS
Axis MY INDIA Predictions	89–101	124–140	0–3	4–8
RESULTS	**134**	**98**	**0**	**0**

Appendix

2017 – MCD Election

26 April 2017

MCD OVERALL (270 Wards) Election held up for 2 Wards (2017)				
PARTY	AAP	BJP	INC	OTHERS
Axis MY INDIA Predictions	23–35	202–220	19–31	2–8
RESULTS	48	181	30	11

26 April 2017

EAST DELHI – 63 Wards (2017)				
PARTY	AAP	BJP	INC	OTHERS
Axis MY INDIA Predictions	6–10	45–51	4–8	0–2
RESULTS	11	47	3	2

26 April 2017

SOUTH DELHI – 104 Wards (2017)				
PARTY	AAP	BJP	INC	OTHERS
Axis MY INDIA Predictions	9–13	79–85	7–11	1–3
RESULTS	16	70	12	6

26 April 2017

NORTH DELHI – 103 Wards (2017)				
PARTY	AAP	BJP	INC	OTHERS
Axis MY INDIA Predictions	8–12	78–84	8–12	1–3
RESULTS	21	64	15	3

Appendix

2017 – Municipal Corporation Election

23 February 2017

BMC – 227 Wards (2017)							
PARTY	SS	BJP+	INC	NCP	MNS	SP	OTHERS
Axis MY INDIA Predictions	86–92	80–88	30–34	3–6	5–7	2–4	5–7
RESULTS	84	82	31	9	7	5	9

23 February 2017

THANE – 131 Wards (2017)					
PARTY	SS	BJP	INC	NCP	OTHERS
Axis MY INDIA Predictions	62–70	26–33	2–6	29–34	0
RESULTS	67	23	3	34	4

23 February 2017

NAGPUR – 151 Wards (2017)					
PARTY	BJP	INC	SS	BSP	OTHERS
Axis MY INDIA Predictions	98–110	35–41	2–4	1–2	3–5
RESULTS	108	29	2	1	11

23 February 2017

PUNE – 162 Wards (2017)					
PARTY	BJP	INC + NCP	SS	MNS	OTHERS
Axis MY INDIA Predictions	77–85	60–66	10–13	3–6	1–3
RESULTS	69	50	10	2	4

Appendix

2017 – Assembly Election

11 March 2017

UTTAR PRADESH (AE 2017) – 403 Seats					
PARTY	BJP+	SP + INC	BSP	RLD	OTHERS
Axis MY INDIA Predictions	251–279	88–112	28–42	2–5	4–11
RESULTS	325	54	19	1	4

11 March 2017

UTTARAKHAND (AE 2017) – 70 Seats				
PARTY	BJP	INC	BSP	OTHERS
Axis MY INDIA Predictions	46–53	12–21	1–2	1–4
RESULTS	57	11	–	2

11 March 2017

PUNJAB (AE 2017) – 117 Seats				
PARTY	AAP	INC	SAD + BJP	OTHERS
Axis MY INDIA Predictions	42–51	62–71	4–7	0–2
RESULTS	20	77	18	2

Appendix

11 March 2017

GOA (AE 2017) – 40 Seats

PARTY	BJP	INC	AAP	SS + MGP + VL	OTHERS
Axis MY INDIA Predictions	18–22	9–13	0–2	3–6	1–3
RESULTS	13	17	–	3	7

11 March 2017

MANIPUR (AE 2017) – 60 Seats

PARTY	INC	BJP	NPF	OTHERS
Axis MY INDIA Predictions	30–36	16–22	3–5	3–6
RESULTS	28	21	4	7

14 December 2017

GUJARAT (AE 2017) – 182 Seats

PARTY	BJP	INC+	OTHERS
Axis MY INDIA Predictions	99–113	68–82	1–4
RESULTS	99	80	3

14 December 2017

HIMACHAL PRADESH (AE 2017) – 68 Seats

PARTY	BJP	INC+	OTHERS
Axis MY INDIA Predictions	47–55	13–20	0–2
RESULTS	44	21	3

Appendix

2018 – Assembly Election

3 March 2018

TRIPURA (AE 2018) – 59 Seats			
PARTY	BJP	LEFT Front	OTHERS
Axis MY INDIA Predictions	44–50	9–15	0–3
RESULTS	43	16	0

3 March 2018

MEGHALAYA (AE 2018) – 59 Seats								
PARTY	INC	NPP	UDP	BJP	HSPDP	PDF	NCP	IND
Axis MY INDIA Predictions	20	14	6	5	5	3	2	4
RESULTS	21	19	6	2	2	4	1	4

15 May 2018

KARNATAKA (AE 2018) – 222 / 224 Seats				
PARTY	INC	BJP	JDS+	OTHERS
Axis MY INDIA Predictions	106–118	79–92	22–30	1–4
RESULTS	78	104	37	3

11 December 2018

MIZORAM (AE 2018) – 40 Seats				
PARTY	MNF	ZPM	INC	OTHERS
Axis MY INDIA Predictions	16–22	8–12	8–12	1–4
RESULTS	26	8	5	1

Appendix

11 Dec 2018

MADHYA PRADESH (AE 2018) – 230 Seats

PARTY	INC	BJP	BSP	OTHERS
Axis MY INDIA Predictions	104–122	102–120	1–3	3–8
RESULTS	114	109	2	5

11 Dec 2018

TELANGANA (GE 2018) – 119 Seats

PARTY	TRS	INC+	BJP	AMIM	OTHERS
Axis MY INDIA Predictions	79–91	21–33	1–3	4–7	0
RESULTS	88	21	1	7	2

11 Dec 2018

CHHATTISGARH (AE 2018) – 90 Seats

PARTY	INC	BJP	JCC + BSP	OTHERS
Axis MY INDIA Predictions	55–65	21–31	4–8	0
RESULTS	68	15	7	0

11 Dec 2018

RAJASTHAN (AE 2018) – 199 / 200 Seats

PARTY	INC	BJP	BSP	OTHERS
Axis MY INDIA Predictions	119–141	55–72	1–3	3–8
RESULTS	101	73	6	19

Appendix

2019 – Assembly Election

ANDHRA PRADESH (AE 2019) – 175 Seats						
PARTY	YSRCP	TDP	JSP	INC	BJP	OTHERS
Axis MY INDIA Predictions	119–135	39–51	1–3	0	0	0–2
RESULTS	**151**	**23**	**1**	**0**	**0**	**0**

ODISHA (AE 2019) – 146 Seats				
PARTY	BJD	BJP	INC	OTHERS
Axis MY INDIA Predictions	89–105	29–43	8–12	0–3
RESULTS	**112**	**23**	**9**	**2**

Appendix

2019 General Election – Exit Poll
Axis My India Delivers Exact Poll – Prediction & Results
Survey Sample Size – 7,42,187

Party-wise Seat Share

Alliance	Prediction	Result*	Party	Prediction	Results*
BJP+ (NDA)	339–365 (Mid Point – 352)	352	BJP	293–316 (Mid Point – 304)	303
INC + (UPA)	77–108 (Mid Point – 92/93)	92	INC	48–65 (Mid Point – 56)	52
OTHERS	69–95	98			

Seat-by-seat Accuracy: 511 (94%) correct predictions out of 542

Alliance / Party-wise Vote Share (%)

Alliance	Party	Party-wise Prediction	Party-wise Results*	Allaince-wise Prediction	Allaince-wise Results*
BJP + (NDA)	BJP	37	37.4	45	44.8
	BJP Allies	8	7.4		
INC + (UPA)	INC	20	19.5	27	26.8
	INC Allies	7	7.3		
OTHERS	Regional	28	28.4	28	28.4

* Source: http://results.eci.gov.in/pc/en/partywise/index.htm

Alliance	Political Parties
BJP+:	BJP, SHS, JDU, AIADMK, SAD, LJP, PMK, AGP, APNA DAL, DMDK, RLP, AJSU, NDPP, BPF, BDJS, AINRC, TMC(M), IND (Sumalatha)
INC+:	CONG, DMK, NCP, RJD, JDS, JMM, IUML, RLSP, CPI, CPI (M), HAM, SWP, JVM, VIP, VCK, RSP, BVA, KC(M), ZPM+CONG, JAP, IND (Navneet Kaur)
Others:	TMC, YSRCP, TRS, LEFT FRONT, SP, TDP, BSP, BJD, RLD, AIMIM, AAP, VBA, NPP, SKM, SDF, JSP, INDP, AIUDF, MNF, NPF

Appendix

2019 – General Election

DAMAN & DIU (GE 2019)	
Axis MY INDIA Predictions	Final RESULTS
BJP	BJP

LAKSHADWEEP (GE 2019)	
Axis MY INDIA Predictions	Final RESULTS
INC	NCP

PUDUCHERRY (GE 2019)	
Axis MY INDIA Predictions	Final RESULTS
INC	INC

ANDAMAN & NICOBAR ISLANDS (GE 2019)	
Axis MY INDIA Predictions	Final RESULTS
BJP	INC

CHANDIGARH (GE 2019)	
Axis MY INDIA Predictions	Final RESULTS
BJP	BJP

Appendix

DADRA & NAGAR HAVELI (GE 2019)	
Axis MY INDIA Predictions	Final RESULTS
BJP	OTHERS

MIZORAM (GE 2019)	
Axis MY INDIA Predictions	Final RESULTS
ZPM/INC	MNF

NAGALAND (GE 2019)	
Axis MY INDIA Predictions	Final RESULTS
INC	NDPP

TRIPURA (GE 2019) – 2 SEATS	
Axis MY INDIA Predictions	Final RESULTS
BJP	BJP
BJP	BJP

SIKKIM (GE 2019)	
Axis MY INDIA Predictions	Final RESULTS
SKM* / SDF	SKM

* Tough Fight – Where margin between first two parties is 3% or less. Party shown first has edge.

Appendix

ARUNACHAL PRADESH (GE 2019) – 2 Seats	
Axis MY INDIA Predictions	Final RESULTS
BJP	BJP
BJP	BJP

MANIPUR (GE 2019) – 2 Seats	
Axis MY INDIA Predictions	Final RESULTS
BJP	BJP
BJP	OTHERS

MEGHALAYA (GE 2019) – 2 Seats	
Axis MY INDIA Predictions	Final RESULTS
INC	INC
NPP	NPP

Appendix

2019 – General Election

JAMMU & KASHMIR (GE 2019) – 6 Seats					
PARTY	BJP	INC	JKNC	PDP	OTHERS
Axis MY INDIA Predictions	2–3	0–1	2–3	0	0
RESULTS	3	0	3	0	0

TAMIL NADU* (GE 2019) – 38/39 Seats			
PARTY	BJP+	INC+	OTHERS
Axis MY INDIA Predictions	0–4	34–38	0
RESULTS	1	37	0

* TN – Vellore Seat Election postponed

TELANGANA (GE 2019) – 17 Seats				
PARTY	TRS	INC	BJP	AIMIM	OTHERS
Axis MY INDIA Predictions	10–12	1–3	1–3	0–1	0
RESULTS	9	3	4	1	0

UTTAR PRADESH (GE 2019) – 80 Seats				
PARTY	BJP+	MGB	INC+	OTHERS
Axis MY INDIA Predictions	62–68	10–16	1–2	0
RESULTS	64	15	1	0

Appendix

| UTTARAKHAND (GE 2019) – 5 Seats ||||
PARTY	BJP	INC	BSP	OTHERS
Axis MY INDIA Predictions	5	0	0	0
RESULTS	5	0	0	0

| WEST BENGAL (GE 2019) – 42 Seats |||||
PARTY	TMC	BJP	INC	CPM/CPI	OTHERS
Axis MY INDIA Predictions	19–22	19–23	0–1	0	0
RESULTS	22	18	2	0	0

| GOA (GE 2019) – 2 Seats |||
PARTY	BJP	INC	OTHERS
Axis MY INDIA Predictions	2	0	0
RESULTS	1	1	0

| MAHARASHTRA (GE 2019) – 48 Seats ||||
PARTY	BJP+	INC+	VBA+	OTHERS
Axis MY INDIA Predictions	38–42	6–10	0	0
RESULTS	41	6	1	0

Appendix

DELHI (GE 2019) – 7 Seats				
PARTY	AAP	BJP	INC	OTHERS
Axis MY INDIA Predictions	0	6–7	0–1	0
RESULTS	0	7	0	0

ODISHA (GE 2019) – 21 Seats				
PARTY	BJD	BJP	INC	OTHERS
Axis MY INDIA Predictions	2–6	15–19	0–1	0
RESULTS	12	8	1	0

PUNJAB (GE 2019) – 13 Seats				
PARTY	BJP+	INC	AAP	OTHERS
Axis MY INDIA Predictions	3–5	8–9	0–1	0
RESULTS	4	8	1	0

RAJASTHAN (GE 2019) – 25 Seats			
PARTY	BJP+	INC	OTHERS
Axis MY INDIA Predictions	23–25	0–2	0
RESULTS	25	0	0

Appendix

HIMACHAL PRADESH (GE 2019) – 4 Seats			
PARTY	BJP+	INC	OTHERS
Axis MY INDIA Predictions	4	0	0
RESULTS	4	0	0

JHARKHAND (GE 2019) – 14 Seats			
PARTY	BJP+	INC+	OTHERS
Axis MY INDIA Predictions	12–14	0–2	0
RESULTS	12	2	0

KARNATAKA (GE 2019) – 28 Seats			
PARTY	BJP	INC+	OTHERS
Axis MY INDIA Predictions	21–25	3–6	0–1
RESULTS	25	2	1

KERALA (GE 2019) – 20 Seats				
PARTY	UDF (INC)	LDF	NDA	OTHERS
Axis MY INDIA Predictions	15–16	3–5	0–1	0
RESULTS	19	1	0	0

Appendix

MADHYA PRADESH (GE 2019) – 29 Seats

PARTY	BJP	INC	OTHERS
Axis MY INDIA Predictions	26–28	1–3	0
RESULTS	28	1	0

ANDHRA PRADESH (GE 2019) – 25 Seats

PARTY	YSRCP	TDP	JSP	INC	BJP	OTHERS
Axis MY INDIA Predictions	18–20	4–6	0–1	0	0	0
RESULTS	22	3	0	0	0	0

ASSAM (GE 2019) – 14 Seats

PARTY	BJP+	INC	AIUDF	OTHERS
Axis MY INDIA Predictions	12–14	0–2	0	0
RESULTS	9	3	1	1

BIHAR (GE 2019) – 40 Seats

PARTY	BJP+	INC	OTHERS
Axis MY INDIA Predictions	38–40	0–2	0
RESULTS	39	1	0

Appendix

CHHATTISGARH (GE 2019) – 11 Seats			
PARTY	BJP	INC	OTHERS
Axis MY INDIA Predictions	7–8	3–4	0–1
RESULTS	9	2	–

GUJARAT (GE 2019) – 26 Seats			
PARTY	BJP	INC	OTHERS
Axis MY INDIA Predictions	25–26	0–1	0
RESULTS	26	0	0

HARYANA (GE 2019) – 10 Seats					
PARTY	BJP	INC	AAP + JJP	INLD	OTHERS
Axis MY INDIA Predictions	8–10	0–2	0	0	0
RESULTS	10	0	0	0	0

Appendix

2019 – Assembly Election

21 Dec 2019

JHARKHAND (AE 2019) – 81 Seats

PARTY	BJP	AJSU	INC + JMM + RJD	JVM	OTHERS
Axis MY INDIA Predictions	22–32	3–5	38–50	2–4	4–7
RESULTS	25	2	47	3	4

24 Oct 2019

MAHARASHTRA (AE 2019) – 288 Seats

PARTY	BJP + SHIV SENA	INC + NCP	VBA	OTHERS*
Axis MY INDIA Predictions	166–194	72–90	0–2	22–32
RESULTS	161	98	0	29

* OTHERS: AIMIM / BVA / CPIM / SP / PWPI / PJP / MNS / JSS / KSP / RSP / SWP / SBP & Independents

24 Oct 2019

HARYANA (AE 2019) – 90 Seats

PARTY	BJP	INC	JJP	OTHERS*
Axis MY INDIA Predictions	32–44	30–42	6–10	6–10
RESULTS	40	31	10	9

* OTHERS: HLP / INLD & Independents

Appendix

2020 – Assembly Election

11 Feb 2020

DELHI (AE 2020) – 70 Seats				
PARTY	AAP	BJP+	INC+	OTHERS
Axis MY INDIA Predictions	59–68	2–11	0	0
RESULTS	**62**	**8**	**0**	**0**

10 Nov 2020

BIHAR (AE 2020) – 243 Seats						
PARTY	NDA	MGB	LJP	GDSF	PDA	OTHERS
Axis MY INDIA Predictions	69–91	139–161	3–5	3–5	0	3–5
RESULTS	**125**	**110**	**1**	**6**	**0**	**1**

NDA – BJP, JDU, VIP & HAM

MGB – RJD, INC, CPI(ML)L, CPI & CPI(M)

Appendix

2021 – Assembly Election

2 May 2021

ASSAM (AE 2021) – 126 Seats			
PARTY	BJP+	INC+	OTHERS
Axis MY INDIA Predictions	75–85	40–50	0–2
RESULTS	75	50	1

2 May 2021

KERALA (AE 2021) – 140 Seats				
PARTY	UDF	LDF	NDA	OTHERS
Axis MY INDIA Predictions	20–36	104–120	0–2	0–2
RESULTS	41	99	0	0

2 May 2021

PUDUCHERRY (AE 2021) – 30 Seats			
PARTY	NDA	UPA	OTHERS
Axis MY INDIA Predictions	20–24	6–10	0–1
RESULTS	16+4*	9	1

* Friendly fight of AINRC (3) and AIADMK (1) candidate as Independent won.

Appendix

2021 – Assembly Election

2 May 2021

TAMIL NADU (AE 2021) – 234 Seats						
PARTY	AIADMK+	DMK+	AMMK+	MNM+	NTK+	OTHERS
Axis MY INDIA Predictions	38–54	175–195	1–2	0–2	0–2	0–1
RESULTS	75	159	0	0	0	0

2 May 2021

WEST BENGAL (AE 2021) – 292 / 294 Seats (2 Seats Election Postponed)			
PARTY	BJP+	TMC+	LEFT+	OTHERS
Axis MY INDIA Predictions	134–160	130–156	0–2	0–1
RESULTS	77	214	1 (RSMP)	0

Acknowledgements

To Chiki Sarkar, for her fascinating sense of spotting a book idea. My thanks to Sweta Dutta for always finding the right words. Editors Nandini Mehta, Keshava Guha and the outstanding Juggernaut team for adding their midas touch to the book.

I am who I am because of the immeasurable contribution of my family, teachers, mentors, friends and well-wishers, not particularly in that order. To all of you, I am forever indebted. Finally, the Axis My India Team, this book, and my heart, belongs to you.

axis MY INDIA | DELIVERING TRUST SINCE 1998

- https://twitter.com/AxisMyIndia
- https://www.facebook.com/Axis-My-India-106178725227620
- https://www.instagram.com/axismyindia1998/

Website https://www.axismyindia.org/
Email amibook@axismyindia.org

A Note on the Author

Pradeep Gupta, a leading name in market research, is India's top psephologist and chairman & managing director of Axis My India, which has successfully predicted forty-four of forty-seven exit polls since 2013. Gupta has a BA in sociology, political science and public administration, a diploma in printing technology and an MBA. He is a graduate of the Owner/President Management Program at Harvard Business School. A first-generation entrepreneur from a dusty village in Madhya Pradesh, Gupta believes his humble beginnings give him an insight into human behaviour. Axis My India's 2019 general election and Haryana assembly election forecasts were the subject of a case study at Harvard Business School.

THE APP FOR INDIAN READERS

Fresh, original books tailored for mobile and for India. Starting at ₹10.

juggernaut.in

1

CRAFTED FOR MOBILE READING

Thought you would never read a book on mobile? Let us prove you wrong.

juggernaut.in

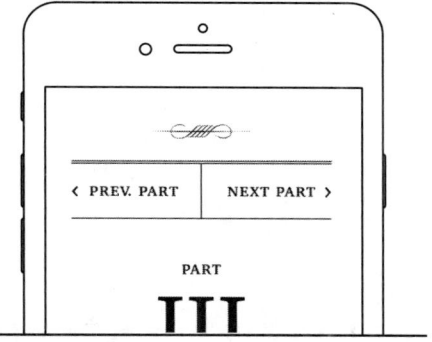

Beautiful Typography

The quality of print transferred to your mobile. Forget ugly PDFs.

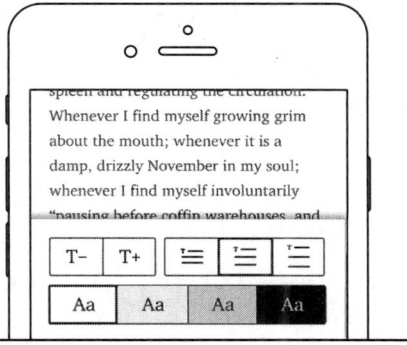

Customizable Reading

Read in the font size, spacing and background of your liking.

juggernaut.in

AN EXTENSIVE LIBRARY

Including fresh, new, original Juggernaut books from the likes of Sunny Leone, Praveen Swami, Husain Haqqani, Umera Ahmed, Rujuta Diwekar and lots more. Plus, books from partner publishers and loads of free classics. Whichever genre you like, there's a book waiting for you.

juggernaut.in

DON'T JUST READ; INTERACT

We're changing the reading experience from passive to active.

juggernaut.in

Ask authors questions

Get all your answers from the horse's mouth. Juggernaut authors actually reply to every question they can.

Rate and review

Let everyone know of your favourite reads or critique the finer points of a book – you will be heard in a community of like-minded readers.

Gift books to friends

For a book-lover, there's no nicer gift than a book personally picked. You can even do it anonymously if you like.

Enjoy new book formats

Discover serials released in parts over time, picture books including comics, and story-bundles at discounted rates. And coming soon, audiobooks.

juggernaut.in

4

LOWEST PRICES & ONE-TAP BUYING

Books start at ₹10 with regular discounts and free previews.

juggernaut.in

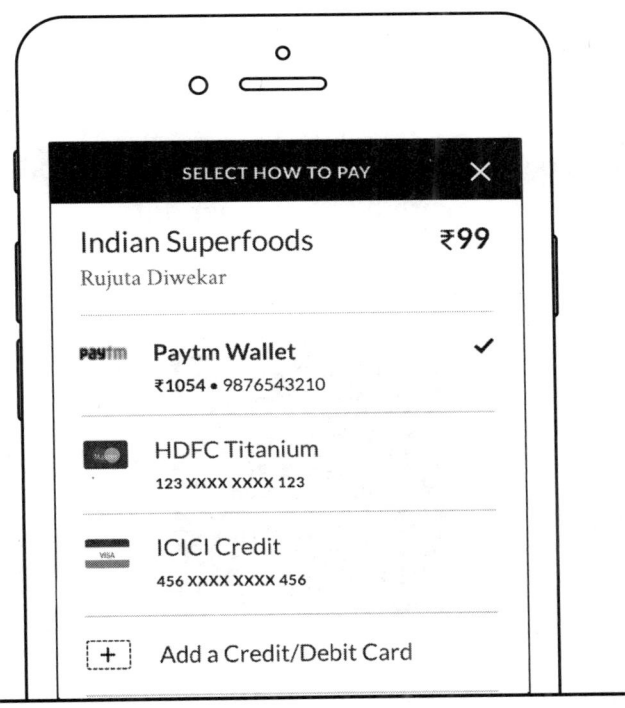

Paytm Wallet, Cards & Apple Payments

On Android, just add a Paytm Wallet once and buy any book with one tap. On iOS, pay with one tap with your iTunes-linked debit/credit card.

To download the app scan the QR Code
with a QR scanner app

For our complete catalogue, visit www.juggernaut.in
To submit your book, send a synopsis and two
sample chapters to books@juggernaut.in
For all other queries, write to contact@juggernaut.in